# 24/7

## WRONGFULLY CONVICTED
## RIGHTFULLY RELEASED

## JONATHAN FLEMING

Book Design by Darshell McAlpine of Boss Lady Press

www.bossladypress.com

Cover Design by Domonique Bowie

www.domoniquedesigns1906.com

Cover Photo by Opia Photography

www.opiaphotography.zenfolio.com

Editor: Janelle Shields

24/7 Wrongfully Convicted Rightfully Released

ISBN: 978-1-7325113-8-5

Library of Congress Control Number: 2020910953

*This book is dedicated first and foremost to God who gave me a second chance at life.*
*My life, not just within the confines of this book, is dedicated to my mother, Patricia Ann Fleming.*
*May you continue to rest in peace.*

# Table of Contents

# ACKNOWLEDGMENTS

How do I say thank you to all the people who have touched my life? There were so many people who played a major role in my success. I will try to include everyone here, but please forgive me if I inadvertently leave anyone out.

First, I want to send a special thank you to my mother in heaven, Patricia Ann Fleming. Mom, you were more than a mother: you were a best friend. You deposited resilience in me, and the will to never give up. I can still hear you say, *Do not allow them folks to pin a murder on you that you didn't commit! I know you didn't do it because you were with me. Trust God always.* Your voice still rings in my ears with the words, *My boy is innocent.* You stuck with me through the rough times and hung around to see the victory. Thank you for looking after my sons and their sons. I am so grateful for the fifteen extra months I had with you before you got your wings. I know you are rocking heaven out.

To my dad, not a day goes by that I don't think of you and wish for just one more time to hear your voice. There is so much we didn't get to say and do, but your love for me was certain. Thank you for being a firm hand.

Shakim, you went to be with the Lord as this book was being written. Brother, you were my friend since we were kids. I never had a biological brother, but God sent you to fit in that space. I pray you are smiling down on me. Another soldier earned his wings.

Kenneth Thompson, it is because of you I can tell this story. Your integrity and passion for true justice caused you to see my case and join the fight to free me. I didn't know when you spoke at my mom's funeral that you did not have much longer. Gone too soon. But your legacy lives on with me and all the other wrongfully convicted men you helped to free.

To my four boys, Jonathan Cherry, Vaughn Peterson, Jamel Stevens, Darius Fleming I love each of you deeply and it's my heart's desire to see each of you reach your fullest potential and change this world for good. I want to acknowledge your mothers who raised you with grace, resilience, patience, and love as single parents. Thank you for all you did to help me while I served my time: taking my calls so I could stay connected to the boys; sending money and cards of encouragement or to just let me know you were thinking of me; passing messages for me to my mom and attorneys. Thank you to Mrs. Brown and Ms. Johnson, my mother-in-laws, who loved me like a son and also made sure they took care of me in any way they could. I cannot forget my godson, Russell William Johnson; you were always there for me and I love you as one of my own.

To my Dream Team, Bob Rahn, Kim Anklin, and Anthony Mayol. Thank you for believing in me, for putting in the work, and seeing me through those trying times. I can't forget the ones that fought my case after my exoneration to assure my compensation.

Last, but always first in my life, I thank God, my Lord and Savior. Even when I didn't know you, you had a plan for my life and you kept me to fulfill that plan.

# I AM NOT A KILLER

G ROWING UP IN THE PROJECTS IN B ROOKLYN IS LIKE living on another planet. The stuff that makes the world go around for those outside the projects doesn't exist in the projects. It's an alternate universe with its own set of rules, and both rule-makers and citizens are subject to the rules. Rules aren't about doing what's right or wrong. They're about survival. Each and every day, you are just trying to stay alive and feed your family. The rule-makers don't have degrees, wear badges, or sit on benches swinging gavels. They rule with an iron fist and fear, with the real power of life and death over everyone who is unlucky enough to live in the projects. It's a place you try to escape, a place you get out from. Getting out is not impossible, but in the minds of the people who live there, it's equal to squeezing through a keyhole. Conditions have to be just right: the right mentors, the emotional stamina, the ability to turn a blind eye, and a chance yellow-brick road to guide you through the dangers on your way out. One slip-up can close the exit door permanently.

Don't misunderstand me. There is an organic flow to the projects too, a way people live together and take care of one another. The stories of the projects' aunties and the bass in the voices of its uncles is its rhythm. It has its innocence in the unmarred hope of its children and even in the strength of those who have raised generations there. History and traditions, whether good or bad, are passed down and life goes on most days, without the drama you see played out on the television. It isn't the life most people dream of, but it is its own type of living.

Unlike many of the kids in the projects, I grew up with two parents, Patricia Ann (Patsy) and Johnny Fleming. My mom had six siblings, three sisters, and three brothers. My dad was the youngest boy of twenty-one kids. My parents met and fell in love in Kingstree, South Carolina. My mom was twenty-one and pregnant with me when she and my dad followed my mom's sisters to Brooklyn, New York. The south has always been a hard place for black people. My parents migrated for the same reason so many black people have: to carve out a better life for their families.

Despite both my parents coming from large families, I was an only child. I was the apple of my mom's eye. She never wanted more than to have me, her son. She poured everything into me and loved me more than I've ever been loved in my life. She was my heart and all of my life I just wanted to take care of her. My mom was my solitary cheering squad and when others abandoned me because the wait was too long, my mother held me down. She never gave up on me.

When we first moved to Brooklyn, we lived in a tiny apartment close to the famous singer Millie Jackson. It was a sign we had moved up when my mom could call back home and say, "Yeah girl, Millie Jackson lives around the corner." I was too young to remember what our life was like then, but both my parents were working and enjoying New York. According to them, life was good.

My dad drove a cement truck back then, but at some point, he developed an affection for alcohol over everything else. Things got so lean that mom started hiding money just so we could have enough to live off of. I was too young to understand what was happening when he stopped working, but he must have gotten injured or something. I don't know if the drinking made him too incapacitated to work, or if he drank because he was too incapacitated to work. Whatever the case, suddenly, he was at home, collecting a Social Security check. That was the way it was for the rest of his life. As I came to understand when I was older, we had to move to the Marcy Projects because we did not have any other options financially.

My very first friend when we moved to Marcy was Anthony "Roach" Sutton. I was only five and too little to be of much help on moving day, but after the long day of moving, I was outside hoping to meet some kids from the neighborhood. No one was out playing. I sat down on the front stairs and swirled ants around with a stick I'd picked up from the patch of dirt that should have been grass. I had been sitting there for a few minutes when I looked up and saw Roach walking over to me. Remember, I was only five and Roach was six. I was excited to see another boy so I introduced myself like any good kid trying to make friends would do. Roach responded by punching me in the face and giving me my first black eye. Welcome to Marcy! Even though our first meeting didn't go well, we became instant friends.

Our little family blended into the projects. My mom and dad were there with me daily when I was growing up. It wasn't common to have a father who lived in the same house in the projects then and I imagine not much has changed. But when I say my dad was there every day, it wasn't an episode of Good Times. I have never doubted his love for me and I know he would have done anything in his power to protect me. But I don't remember ever having one conversation with him about how to be a man, how to treat a woman, or even how to stay out of trouble. When I would get in trouble, he was the first one to get on me. He was hard on me and didn't hesitate to wear me out if I got caught doing something wrong, but he had his own challenges and sometimes those challenges got in the way of his parenting. He would say to my mother, "If that boy ends up in jail, I ain't going to see him." He kept that promise.

I loved my dad like any boy loves his dad, but he had a drinking problem and it hurt me to see him hurting himself. I remember living on the first floor and having my dad sneak into my room so people could pass him liquor through my bedroom window. He would give money to anybody willing to bring him something to drink without my mom knowing. But I don't know what he was thinking. It wasn't like Mom wouldn't find out when he showed up tipsy. I guess he was trying to keep from hearing her mouth until he had completed his mission.

To make matters worse, when I was nine, I caught my dad cheating on my mom, and I told her about it. How jacked up is that? I was a nine-year-old boy witnessing my dad messing around on my mom and then carrying the burden of having to tell my mother.

You have to know something about Patsy Fleming. She was not here for my dad's foolishness. The night I told her about my dad and Lana, she let her rage bake real good while she braided her hair in cornrows straight to the back and rubbed her face down with Vaseline. Those of you that come from a different upbringing may not know what it means when someone from the hood rubs their face down with Vaseline, but even at nine years old, I knew my mom was planning to give somebody a good old-fashioned ass whipping, and the Vaseline made sure she didn't get scratched up in the process.

She was huffing and puffing and mumbling under her breath like a madwoman while she braided her hair. I asked her what she was doing. She was so pissed she cursed me out, telling me in so many words to "take my behind to bed." I told you my mother was my everything, so I had to know what was going down. I hid in the living room behind the couch until I saw her leave the house. I left right out behind her, but she was so fixated on her mission that she didn't even notice me following her.

Lana lived in another building in the same projects. When my mom made it out of our building, she saw Lana sitting outside on the stairs in front of her building. Before that lady knew what was happening, Patsy Fleming swooped down on her like a fire-breathing dragon and brought that woman so much pain. Lana was no match for my mother's beat down. I was screaming and crying so much that my mom stopped beating Lana long enough to look up at me. To this day, I think that's the only thing that saved Lana from dying on the front stoop that night. My mother told her in no uncertain terms to leave my dad alone, and that was the end of that.

One of my most vivid memories of my dad was having some guy I didn't know come to my door and tell me that my dad was outside and needed help. When I got outside, my dad was holding on to the fence, so drunk that he was struggling to hold himself up. It's like his fingers were just as lost as his legs, unable to grasp the rungs of the fence and too weak to support his body. He couldn't stand, and I had to get to him before he was laid out on the sidewalk. You can't know what it's like for a son to watch his dad while other people watch him humiliate himself. I don't know if I was more embarrassed for myself because he was my father or if I was more embarrassed for him because he couldn't help himself. The currents of love and shame shouldn't be allowed to flow through a person at the same time.

My dad and I didn't have 'father-son talks,' so I

don't know what made him want to drink so much. I also don't know why he couldn't stop, despite the damage he was doing to himself and to the family. No matter how much we struggled, he couldn't break his addiction. My mom took the twenty-five dollars a day she made cleaning houses and put it with whatever my dad didn't spend on liquor to make things happen for us day after day.

My mom told me she stayed with my dad because she knew that if she left him, he wouldn't make it more than a couple of days. They were more like room-mates. I never knew them to be intimate. My mom even had a boyfriend later in their relationship. I wasn't mad about her having someone else. I felt she deserved happiness. I was glad she had found some joy.

Mom kept us together. She cleaned white folks' houses to pay the bills and keep us fed. I would go with her to clean houses that seemed like mansions to a kid like me from the projects. We could've fit our whole apartment in one room. My mom busted her ass scrubbing floors and cleaning toilets for less than minimum wage. I hated seeing her working like that and not being able to have the things she deserved. She was our family's anchor. It's true she spoiled me and tried to make sure I didn't want for anything, at least not the basic things a boy needs. But I wanted more, and I wanted to give her more.

Despite all my mom did, she couldn't keep me away from the influence of the streets. I was known as Hook in the projects, which was a childhood tease that stuck. Some kid in second grade started calling me 'hook head' and the rest of the kids started pointing and laughing, saying, "hook head, hook head." I felt like every child feels when they're the butt of the joke, but the name took on new meaning as I got older and begin finding ways to ease my mother's burden.

When I was thirteen, I joined a little league baseball team called the Dodgers, named after the Brooklyn Dodgers. I played first base and pitched pretty well, too. I was good at baseball. It was the first time in my life that I considered things could be different, that my life could go a different way. For a while, I just knew I would be a professional baseball player, but life in the projects pisses on a lot of dreams, and if you aren't careful or perceptive, you stay stuck.

It was the little league kids that introduced me to weed. Not that I didn't know about weed beforehand, but I didn't start smoking it until I started playing baseball. Then we added some Old English 800 malt liquor, which could probably power a Boeing 747 from New York to Japan on one bottle. We thought we were doing something serious by smoking weed and drinking malt liquor. Baseball went from being something I dreamed would give me a chance at a positive future to a way to get into mischief, although I didn't see it that way then.

I added cigarettes to the weed and Old English. Mom wasn't tripping about the weed, but she was not feeling the cigarettes. She hated the smoking, but she let me do it for a while without nagging me about it. One night when I came home, she had placed a pack of cigarettes and a cigar on the kitchen table. When I opened the door and saw her sitting at the kitchen table watching the door like she was waiting for Satan to walk through it, I paused before closing the door. I thought to myself "What did I do?" Mom motioned for me to come sit down next to her at the table. She patted the chair in front of her. I said to myself, "I must have really messed up." I was racking my brain trying to think about what I could have done to make her act calm but deadly as I slowly walked over to the chair. I could not come up with anything. I sat down slowly, nervous that she would start swinging. But she didn't.

She lit the cigar and said, "Take a hit of this since you want to act like you're grown. If you want to smoke so bad then let me help you." I relaxed, realizing that she was not going to hit me. The cigar did not scare me. Hell, I was looking forward to smoking it. I shrugged my shoulders and took the first drag off the cigar. I knew nothing about smoking cigars, but I figured it wasn't that much different from smoking cigarettes, so I hit it like you would a cigarette. Before I knew it, I was gagging and choking, but I would not be made a fool of. I kept choking and gagging and dragging my way through that cigar until my chest felt like I swallowed a volcano, all while mom sat there watching me like an eagle about to snatch up a mouse. My body filled with the cigar smoke as my stomach churned. It took a few seconds for my mind to register that my stomach was getting ready to give up its contents. I took off running to the bathroom feeling the surge and wondering if I would make it. My eyes watered and my head thumped as my stomach heaved. I hung over the toilet and vomited until I was exhausted.

I got up and stumbled back into the kitchen holding my stomach, sure I would have to hug the toilet again at any minute. My mom had not moved from her chair at the kitchen table. She looked up at me, slightly leaning her head to the right with a matter-of-fact expression and said, "Boy, I don't ever want you to smoke another cigar or cigarette as long as you are living and breathing. Our people cropped tobacco in the South, and it killed more of us than it ever helped. You understand me?" I said through groans, "yes, ma'am." It was a long time before I smoked again.

It was hard to steer clear of the smoking and drinking when my house was the neighborhood party house. We had card parties every weekend, and I got good at playing. I played well enough to keep up with the adults. It was another way to make money. Mom made fish dinners, which we also sold to make extra money. My aunts and uncles would come to the parties, and I think it was after one of these parties that my Uncle Shorty gave me my first gun. Uncle Shorty married my aunt Flossie, or Aunt Toot as we called her; she was my mom's oldest sister. The gun was a nickel-plated thirty-two. I know I paid him for it, but he had his chest stuck out because he was the person who gave me my first gun. I know what you're thinking. What grown man would give a fourteen-year-old boy a gun?

Let's pause here to get some perspective. It's easy for us to get caught up in our way of doing things or to have such limited tunnel vision that we cannot comprehend another person's frame of reference or point of view. We are all products of our environment and the influences we've had over a lifetime. But I am asking you to put all that aside and try to see the world through the eyes of someone who lived in my environment.

I don't know why Uncle Shorty sold me the gun, but I know he loved me and the intention wasn't to hurt me. Nor was he planning on me hurting anyone else. If I had to guess why he let me buy the gun, it was probably because he lost a lot of money that night playing cards and the only way to get some of it back was to sell me the gun. My mom found the gun, but there was only so much she could do to keep me from using it or getting another one.

I didn't have many upstanding men in my life. Drug dealers like Baldy and Son ran the Marcy Projects. They were my idols. I wanted to be like them and have what they had. They sold drugs, but they helped mothers and grandmothers put food on the table. They talked to the young guys about staying in school and helped coach some of the talented athletes, encouraging them to go to college. To me, they were larger than life, and even though they both succumbed to the power of the dope game, one killed and the other addicted, that happened long after they had left an impression on me. I didn't think about going to college or getting a good job. I came from Marcy, and that meant I had to find whatever means necessary to elevate myself. I did what I saw being done. If I was going to help my mom and enjoy the finer things in life, I was going to have to take them.

I committed my first robbery when I was fourteen or fifteen years old, with the gun I bought from Uncle Shorty. I was in tenth grade and attending a unique maritime school that had a regular school campus and then a campus on a boat that docked on the Hudson River. I wasn't a great student, not because I wasn't smart. I just wasn't interested. I was distracted by the allure of things. I wanted things and I couldn't see how school would help me get them. Neither my mom nor my dad graduated high school, so it was important to her that I did. But I wasn't focused on that.

One afternoon, I spotted a gold necklace around the neck of another student. I snatched that gold necklace right off his neck in the stairwell at school. The next day, I found out that people knew it was me who had done the robbery and that some of his people were looking for me. I didn't go back to that school but I got transferred to another school.

It wasn't long after I got to the new school that I became friends with this kid named Michael. Me and Michael robbed this Italian dude of his gold Jesus-head medallion. Yeah, I stole Jesus too. Michael got picked up the next day but I didn't go back to school until two days later with my mom. When the police came to question me, I acted like I didn't know anything about what they were talking about. Michael ended up getting released, but I was charged with the robbery. Michael was scared straight and never committed another crime. He went on to make a great career for himself in the military. I ended up with five years of probation and got better at robbing.

I did eventually graduate from high school, and I even tried college to please my mother. But college didn't have the immediate financial gratification that my current occupation did. Committing robberies became a way of life. At first, it was about getting things I didn't have. But somewhere along the line, it changed; it became about the adrenaline and the power.

I will not blame my tendency for taking things that didn't belong to me on the projects, or my dad, or whatever other reason people give for their behavior. I own my past. At the time, my thought was that I had to make money in whatever way I could. I learned that I could take what I wanted, when I wanted. I was good at it. I started robbing to make a better life for myself and those close to me. But eventually, it got to where I robbed when I didn't have to and took things I didn't need from anyone who had it. I was never scared, nor did I think about dying or killing anyone. The only thing on my mind was getting whatever I had my eye on.

I graduated from snatch and grabs to much more lucrative means of getting money. I ran a check scam, or should I say I stole checks and sold them to a fence who gave me back a percentage of the value of each check. The mailman would leave his cart outside while he delivered mail to the different buildings. While he was inside putting mail in the individual mailboxes, I would grab as many bundles of mail as I could from his mail cart and run off. I would go through the mail, taking out all the Social Security checks. If I got $60K worth of checks, the fence would give me a third. I did this for about six months until the Feds got hip to the scam and the fence set me up.

The fence contacted me to change our drop-off location for our next exchange. I should have known then that something was off. I met him at the new location and got into his car. He was jumpy and I felt like I should get out of there without making the transaction. I ignored that feeling and finished our deal as normal. As soon as the cash changed hands, the Feds were on us. The fence had been wearing a wire for the Feds, which he agreed to do so he could get less time. I was supposed to be his scapegoat.

Stealing mail is a federal crime. They arrested me but let me go the same day. I was charged with possession of treasury checks and was given five years' probation since my crime was not violent. Undeterred by my arrest and conviction, I thought to myself, '*I just need to change my hustle.*' A couple of months after being convicted of that crime, I violated my probation in grand style.

I had some mentors in the projects that probably weren't the sort of people you would look up to, but they helped me develop my skill. Cloud was one of those mentors. He showed me another way to get what

I needed. He was an ex-con who had gone to prison for two-and-a-half years for robbery. But he was back on the streets and looking for someone younger to help him. He recruited me and my partner, Whites. Cloud figured we wouldn't get as much time if we got caught because of how young we were. He schooled us on how to stake out a location and understand the right time to make a move. At first, he would case out the people making money bag drops at the bank. Once he knew a person's schedule, me and Whites would use the information he gave us to rob folks of their money bags before they entered the bank. Whites would wait on the motorcycle nearby. I would approach the target with my gun aimed and say, "Don't make the newspapers tomorrow." Once I got the money, Whites would pull around, I would jump on the bike and we would make our get-away.

After a while, we got hip to Cloud using us; we started skimming from the robberies. We told Cloud that we got less than we did and pocketed the difference. Eventually, we cut him out altogether. We got so good at it that we had our own operation. We became 'robbing contractors' for the projects. If you needed a little something extra, we would set you up to do a job for us and share the profits with you.

We only ran into a problem once. We were riding away on the motorcycle from a robbery when the guy we robbed shot at us. So many robberies and nobody had ever tried to fight back. This guy gave up the money with no problem. But as we rode away, he started shooting. We got away from him, but on the way back to the projects, there were three ladies trying to cross the street when they saw us coming. Two of the ladies waited, but one of them tried to outrun the motorcycle. Whites tried to swerve to keep from hitting her but it was too late. Whites struck her and we both fell off the bike.

We jumped up and started running in different directions, leaving the bike in the middle of the street. I was able to make my way back to the projects. A crowd caught up with Whites and gave him a beating for hitting the lady. They broke his leg bad enough that he had to stay in the hospital. I still had the money bag, but I was waiting for Whites to get out of the hospital before I opened it.

That night, my wrist hurt so badly that my girl-friend had to take me to the hospital. I had broken my wrist when I fell off the motorcycle, but I guess the adrenaline kept me from noticing until that night. When Whites got out of the hospital, we opened the money bag together. It was one of the biggest paydays we'd ever had. Whites and I were a pair, him with a cast on his leg and me with a cast on my arm. That didn't stop us from handling business though. The next week we did another money bag robbery, casts and all.

Whites was already waiting to be sentenced while we were doing all these robberies and eventually, he went to jail. We had a fool-proof system. With Whites locked up, I tried to duplicate our success with a different crew and a different vehicle. We had been casing this businessman moving money from his store to the bank in a Hasidic Jewish neighborhood. On the day we were set to do the job, we watched the man leave the bank. Whites and I never allowed a mark to make it to their vehicle, but this new crew didn't know the routine and let the man get into his car.

Now we had to follow him. He parked in front of his business and went into the lobby. I dropped the crew off and watched them as they ran into the lobby and wrestled the money bag from the man. I drove a short distance around the block and waited so we could get away quickly. They grabbed the money, ran around the block, and jumped into the car. Everything was going well, up to the point where we tried to get out of the neighborhood. I was on a one-way street, trying to floor it. Just as I was getting up to speed, a UPS truck driving the wrong way down the one-way came right toward us. I couldn't drive forward, so I tried to speed backward. But I couldn't move; the traffic was too heavy.

Those Hasidic Jews had their own policing system and an information hotline that allowed them to shut the neighborhood down in minutes so no one could get in or out. I kept trying street after street while the crew sat in the car yelling, "Man hurry up and get us out of here." There was no way to escape the neighborhood because word had traveled fast through the tight community that we had robbed one of their own. Vehicles and angry crowds blocked every street. We tried to ditch the car and run for it, everyone in a different direction. BAD IDEA!!!

The crowds caught up with each of us. The entire community gave us a good old-fashioned beat down. I was on the ground getting kicked, punched, stomped, and hit with anything the mob could find. I lay there trying to protect my head and back and stomach and arms from blow after blow as I looked up into righteously seething faces of little boys, grandmas, old men, and young women. I got a glimpse of people pouring out of doors and appearing from between buildings, each with their eyes set on getting a piece of me. I was relieved when the police took me away. When I saw one of my partners, I realized my mob had gone easy on me. My partner was pretty lumped up. I was sentenced to two to four years for reckless endangerment. It was the first time I was sent to serve time upstate. The rest of the crew were sentenced to four to eight years for robbery.

People asked me what I did with all the money from the robberies. We spent it. We wore the jewelry and gave it away. We didn't value it because we had so much of it. The truth is, we didn't save a penny. We didn't think about saving because if money got low, we could just commit another robbery. We partied hard day and night. We stayed out in the clubs late, drinking and getting high and doing whatever we wanted to do. There was angel dust, weed, and cocaine. Some folks did heroin and crack. Then we went home, slept it off, and started all over again the next day. If my family needed something, I took care of it.

I had to be creative to help my mother. She didn't know exactly what I was doing for money at first, but she knew it was illegal. She didn't want to know, and I wasn't about to tell her. She was still the love of my life, and I wanted to lighten her load. But initially, she wouldn't take the money knowing I got it illegally. I had to find other ways to provide for her, like have other people bring her things or just leave things for her. I made sure my friends were taken care of too, and I even took care of one of my girlfriend's ex-boyfriends. Robbing was my job. I went to work faithfully to make sure I took care of my family. We were all able to enjoy some of the finer things in life.

I was never a killer, and even though I used a weapon to commit robberies, it was just to create fear and control the situation. Even when we were being shot at, I didn't shoot back. I had a gun, but it never occurred to me to use it to end someone's life.

## 2

# TOO MANY WRONG TURNS

IF YOU HAD ASKED ME AT ANY POINT IN MY YOUNG LIFE if I was going to turn to a life of crime, I would have answered with a resounding 'No!' I definitely didn't see myself going to jail or prison. Those things probably aren't part of anyone's life plan. I can sit here and tell you 'it just happened that way,' but that would be a crock of you know what, and since we're being honest, I didn't have a plan past making money.

Making money was my plan A, B, and C. It remained that way for most of my life, even after I went to prison. For forty-nine years I chased green paper, doing whatever I could come up with to get it. If one thing failed, then I tried something new. If something new didn't work, then something different might. The only thing that mindset rewarded me with was a prisoner number.

I was sent to Elmira, a prisoner reception facility, where convicts were housed while they waited to be transferred to the prison where they would serve their full sentence. They assigned me to Collins Correctional Facility. I was all packed and ready to go to Collins when my transfer was canceled to allow the Feds time to pick me up for violating my probation on the check scam.

The Feds took me to see the judge who sentenced me to one year of federal time, which I had to serve after serving the two to four years for the reckless endangerment. They took me back to Elmira and then I was reassigned to Orleans Correctional Facility instead of Collins. I served twenty-four months at Orleans before the parole board gave me a release date. They scheduled my release for February, but I knew I wasn't going home. The Feds were coming to pick me up so I could serve the one year of federal time for the probation violation.

Before my scheduled release from Orleans, they sent me to Lincoln, a pre-release facility. On my scheduled release date, the Feds did not come to pick me up. The state couldn't hold me at Lincoln while they waited for the Feds to transport me once my state time had been served, so they released me and I went home. Two days later, while I was at the house with my mom, my girlfriend and my three-year-old son, Jamel, there was a knock at the front door. My mom came to my bedroom door and said, "I don't know what's going on, but the police are here." When I looked out the window, the police were ready outside, just in case I tried to run. I went to the front door, fearing what would happen next.

I hadn't been home long enough to get into any trouble. The police came in and told me they were there to pick me up on the federal probation violation. The police officers were not harsh like the police officers I was accustomed to. They told me they had made a mistake by releasing me and they were there to pick me up on the probation violation. They were kind enough to take me to the judge to see if he would reconsider and put me on probation.

I asked them not to handcuff me in front of Jamel, and they didn't. Instead, they took me in the hallway and put the handcuffs on me and then escorted me to the car. I went to court and waited until the end of the day to see the judge. When the bus came to transport prisoners, they called my name. I told them I was waiting to see the judge, but the judge wouldn't see me. The judge told the officers he didn't need to see me because I had already been sentenced. The guards transported me with the rest of the prisoners back to jail.

That night, I was so heated; I got into a fight with another inmate. I was making phone calls trying to let my family know what was going. They had seen the police take me away, but they didn't know where I was or what had happened to me. An inmate waiting to use the phone got agitated waiting on me to finish my calls. I had been on the phone longer than I was supposed to, but I didn't care. The inmate walked up on me yelling, "Get off the phone!" I smashed his face in with the phone and spent my first forty-five days of federal time in the box. I did a total of nine months and seventeen days in federal prison.

When I came home from prison in 1987, the game had changed. Selling drugs had become the latest money maker. I didn't know the first thing about drugs. I was trying to figure out my next hustle, and drugs were a good possibility. There was no way I was going to take a regular job. I needed to find something fast to make big money. I would have been a fool to fall back on robbery since that was the first thing police would expect me to do. I'd only been out about two weeks when I was in the parking lot talking to Spank, a friend of mine, and this dude I knew named Sha'kim pulled up in a champagne gold BMW. He was in the driver's seat, and this Dominican guy they called Julio was driving.

I wasn't used to seeing cars like that. When I'd gone away, everyone was driving around in Cadillacs. Crack brought a whole different level of wealth to the projects. Sha'kim rolled down the window, surprised to see that I was out of prison. He wanted to know what I was getting into that night. I got in the car with them since I didn't have anything else going on. Julio took me shopping that same night, even though we had just met. He bought me clothes and a coat to celebrate my prison release. I wanted to be able to roll the way he was rolling, to drive what he was driving, to spend money like he was spending money. I didn't know anything about the drug game, but before the night was over, I was committed to building a drug empire.

Julio showed me how to set-up. I started out working for him. He would give me $5,000 of product, and I would sell it. He had a guy who was selling for him in Marcy, but that guy liked to use the product. It took him four or five days to move the product because he was too busy getting high. I came in and moved the product in two days. Within a week, Julio was giving me $10,000 of product, which took me three to four days to sell. Then he started giving me a kilo which I also moved in record time.

Julio paid me $2,500 a week, but I've always been entrepreneurial-minded, even if it wasn't aimed in the right direction. When I saw how much money I was making for Julio versus how much he was paying me, I started thinking about how I could run my own show. I'd known Julio for a couple of months, but the idea of being my own boss piqued my interest. I had already hired Spank and expanded from selling product out of one building to selling out of two. I went from making $15,000 a week to $30,000 a week within two months. Within four months, I was making $8,000 to $10,000 a day.

When I told Julio I needed more than $2,500 for the amount of work I was producing, he told me the only way he would pay me more was if I got rid of Spank. I brought Spank in to help expand our territory. Julio liked the idea expansion, but he did not want to pay two people to do it. Basically, he was offering to give me Spank's share instead of increasing my share. I refused.

I made an enemy that day, and he would patiently wait to come for me later, but if I was nothing else, I was loyal to my friends. Turns out, Spank didn't share this same affinity for loyalty. I went to Spank expecting he would hear me out, and we would come up with a plan to start our business. I was surprised to hear him say he would be working for Julio exclusively. Julio had told him that I was trying to cut him out. I didn't care about Julio trying to circumvent me, but I couldn't believe that Spank believed him.

That was the end of both my partnership with Julio and my friendship with Spank. I would not take any more product from Julio, and I began looking for a supplier, which I had no problem finding. I paced myself and gradually became one of the biggest drug dealers in the Williamsburg Projects. I used two apartments in the projects as my base. Before I knew it, I was making more money than I'd ever had.

I don't know if it was because I was older and less impulsive, but I was much better at selling drugs than I ever was at robbing. No matter how much the police tried to shake me down, I was never arrested. No drugs were ever found on my person or in my proximity. I was stopped with curious amounts of cash more than once, but I honestly think the police were just lining their pockets. None of the money they took off me ever made it into evidence. They used me like an ATM. I can see the cops saying, "Hey, my car needs new tires. Let's shakedown Hook so we can get some money."

No matter what you think personally about what I did for a living back then, I want dismantle the image you have of drug dealers. Yes, selling most drugs is illegal in this country without a license. A drug dealer's life is much like that of any entrepreneur. You wake up every morning and review the previous day's profits. You capitalize expenses and work with constituents to make deals. You have to stave off overzealous competition looking to move you out of the market. You review profit and losses, and you have to manage teams, which includes hiring and firing. You must also have a sustainable growth strategy and long-term plans to expand your business into multiple markets.

The major difference between drug dealing and entrepreneurship, besides the fact that it is illegal, is that entrepreneurs seldom have to worry that family, friends, and foes are all trying to kill you so they can capitalize on what you've accumulated. Like other businesses, there is always someone in your organization that is looking to get over, someone who thinks the person at the top is getting too much profit and that they deserve the same benefits as the owner. I was constantly having to move people out of my organization for stealing in one form or another. I never killed any of them. I just hired someone new.

Darryl "Black" Rush and I were both from Marcy. His brothers and I are around the same age, but he was a little younger than me. A lot of the younger guys looked up to the older guys who had come home from upstate prison. He saw me making money and wanted to get in with me. I took him to Williamsburg with me to show him how the operation ran and gave him a position.

We hired people who smoked crack to sell it in the street and paid them $100 a shift. A shift was three to four hours. Black was the runner; he would go to the stash house where we stored the product. To set up the stash house, I hired a lady named Connie who allowed us to use her apartment. No drugs were sold in the stash house. It was only used as a storage facility. Black was responsible for getting the product from the stash house and distributing it to the workers. Once the workers sold the product, Black would pick up the money and take it back to the stash house. Then he would pick up more product and distribute it for the next shift.

I actually didn't notice at first that money was going missing because we were making so much of it. But about six months after Black started working for me, a lady who bought drugs from one of the workers came to me and told me that Black was getting high off the product. She told me which apartment he was in, and I went there to find him getting high. When I saw him, I grabbed him up and we got into an altercation. He got ready to come at me and my guy stopped him. I told him he could not work for me anymore. I meant it.

I'd see him around after that and we'd speak, but

we didn't have any other interaction. I think he was embarrassed by what had happened. We'd had words and parted ways. Yes, I was pissed, but I never wished him dead over it. I'd never taken a life to that point, and I wasn't planning on starting. We stopped talking and went on with our separate lives.

I only wanted to kill a man once, and I make no apologies for it. I came home from my girlfriend's house and as I walked up to the apartment, I could see my godson Russell (William Johnson) sitting on the bench directly in front of the apartment with a full view of everyone coming and going. We talked for a quick second and then I went towards the apartment.

As soon I walked in, I could see my father face down on the kitchen floor, with the bottom half of his body extended into the living room. I ran to him, calling out his name. "Dad!" He made groaning sounds but didn't say anything or move. I looked around and saw to my right that my bedroom door was open. The room had been ransacked. I went to the sink and grabbed a knife because I wasn't sure if someone was still in the house. I went through the house checking for who could have done this. I ran back to my father and turned him over. I was calling to him, but he just moaned; he couldn't answer. I could tell he had been hit with something in the face because the area around his nose was swollen. He must have struggled with someone. I called 911 then ran outside to ask Russell if he had seen anyone leaving the house. He told me he'd seen Will, my dad's friend, leave just ten minutes earlier.

No other room had been touched except for mine. Whoever had been there had gone through everything, my closets, and my drawers. My stuff was everywhere. I had a jewelry box full of gold jewelry, and it was gone. I also had a water bottle, the five-gallon kind used for water dispensers, where I kept dollars bills. It had been cut open and all the dollar bills were gone. When the police came, instead of being concerned about my father, they taunted me saying, "This is what happens when you sell drugs." I went to the hospital with my dad, but before leaving I called my mom. She met us there.

The police questioned me, but I didn't tell them what Russell had told me about Will. I was hell-bent on catching him myself, and I planned to show him the same mercy he'd shown my dad.

I didn't know that much about Will. He'd moved to the projects about six months before I came home from prison in 1987. He ran errands for my dad, and he lived with my son's best friend. His girlfriend's brother, Earl, was in jail, and I gave Will money to take to Earl to help while he was locked up. Will wasn't from Marcy, and wasn't as familiar with our family as everyone else was, but we treated him just like family. My dad had considered him a friend and had been nothing but kind to him. It's still hard to imagine how he could bash my dad like that.

My dad was rushed to the Woodhall hospital and eventually regained consciousness, but he was even more out of it than he was when he was drinking. He was talking but kept calling me Eddie, which was his brother's name. He didn't even know who I was.

The doctor at Woodhall Hospital seemed anxious to discharge him, but I knew he was in no condition to be released. They discharged him anyway, and we took him from Woodhall Hospital to King's County Hospital because we knew he was not doing well. He had an MRI at King's County Hospital, and the doctor saw two blood clots in his brain. The clots were caused by the beating. My dad had to be rushed into surgery. The doctors told us that the first seventy-two hours were the most critical. If he could make it through seventy-two hours, then he had a good chance of recovering.

When he came out of surgery, his head was shaved, and he had staples across the top front of his head from one side to the other. I teared up seeing him that way. I tried talking to him, but he still didn't know who I was. Mom and I stayed with him for a long time, but we finally went home once he was stable and tried to sleep. Family and friends came over to comfort us and as usual, we played cards and made food. Sometime during the night, the hospital called; my dad didn't make it. We rushed back to the hospital in shock.

Knowing Will had done this to my dad made me angrier than I had ever been before. My first thought was to find the man who killed my dad and return the favor. Somehow, this man who was as common to the neighborhood as smothered pork chops and collard greens, was nowhere to be found. He'd left his girl-friend right after the assault and was pretty much a ghost after that. He didn't look back to check on his girlfriend or on anyone else. Will was in the wind, and you know how hard it is to chase the wind.

I ran into Will about two months later when we were both put into a lineup. The police picked me up on suspicion that I had robbed a bodega. Hook was not a bodega robber. This was just another form of the shakedown. The police could not pin a drug charge on me, so they tried to get me for a robbery. I had long since given up robbing in favor of more profitable exploits, and they knew it.

As I stood for the lineup, in walked Will. He looked up at me and then quickly put his head down, refusing to make eye contact. I wanted him to see my fury and to know that I was coming for him, but he never looked my way. Neither one of us was picked out of the lineup. Will was released first, but they made me wait thirty minutes before they let me go. I was anxious to get out because I wanted to put my hands on Will. When they released me, I looked all over the neighborhood for him. People told me he was in this project or that project, and I went to every location like a dog on a hunt to find him, but he never resurfaced. Thirty years later, and I still don't know what became of Will. The truth is, if I had found Will back then, I probably would have ended his life for what he'd done to my dad.

I seldom talk about what happened to my dad. It's too hard to see the blame on people's faces after they hear the story. The voices of the police officers echo in my head, "This is what happens when you sell drugs." What they don't know about is the guilt I carry like a pack mule. I avoid talking about it so I don't have to feel that guilt. It still breaks my heart. I still feel like it was my fault.

Will was hoping to score big by breaking into my house. I don't think he would have killed my dad for his SSI check. I wrestle with the idea that my dad was probably trying to keep Will out of my room, to keep him from taking anything from me, and Will beat the hell out of my dad just to get into my room. Once my dad was down, Will had to work quickly to get what he wanted. I missed all of this by ten minutes, but I swear if I had been there, this whole story would have turned out differently. As I said, I'm not a killer, and I guess God wanted to keep it that way.

People have said that maybe I deserved the twenty-four years and seven months I did for a crime I did not commit after learning of the crimes I did commit. The police could not charge me for the stuff I did, so they got me for something I could not have done. I'm not trying to convince anyone of what I did or didn't deserve. What's more, I know who I was back then, but I also know who I am today. I have given myself permission to stop apologizing for the crimes I committed and the ones I didn't because at the end of the day, I paid a grip for all of it. People's perception is what they have to reconcile.

3

# IRON CLAD ALIBI

I WAS LOCKED UP TWENTY-FOUR YEARS FOR A MURDER I didn't commit, but I was not the main victim in this whole scheme. Darryl "Black" Rush was the real victim. He lost his life over nothing. That I was forced to take the rap for it was just another tragedy that came out of the loss of his life. Black was someone I'd known well for years. At one point, we were like family. Our mothers were close friends too, and our families were intertwined.

I'm not going to spend this chapter talking about the crooked Brooklyn Police Department. It's a well-documented fact that some of the worst criminals wore badges and were licensed to carry guns. Though I have worked through much of what they did to me, it still stings a bit when I think about how much Detective

Kenney wanted me in jail. He and I were well acquainted; it seems he spent his waking hours trying to find any way he could to put me behind bars.

I don't know at what point Detective Kenney decided he would frame me for Black's murder. When Black was killed, Detective Kenney ratcheted up his attempts to arrest me and went about doing whatever he could to make me the person responsible for the killing. Much of what I know now about how far he went to bend and twist the law, I found out after I had already been convicted. It's been thirty years since I was convicted, and I'm still finding out bits of information.

Recently, I learned that a piece of paper with the names of the real killers written in Detective Kenney's scribble had been in the file the whole time. My lawyers requested the records for my civil case after I was released from prison and right there, in the file, was the hand-written note. I will do my best to put the pieces together in a way that you can understand, but imagine me being confronted repeatedly over the last thirty years as the story unfolded little by little.

Again, you may say that it was Karma that I was charged since I was committing other crimes. But if I got what I was due, what is Karma serving up for Detective Kenney and the rest of the Brooklyn judicial system? They made a mockery of the legal system.

They let Black's killers get away, they destroyed the lives of numerous people to satisfy their bravado, and they cost taxpayers money. Why? Because they were fanatical about imprisoning me.

Detective Kenney knew right away who killed Black, but he set about pinning the murder on me for reasons I still struggle to comprehend. Maybe you can make more sense of it than I can. In any case, the story starts here.

I had taken my family on an all-expense-paid trip to Disneyland for my son's ninth birthday. Along with one of my girlfriends, Valerie, my mom, my sons, Jonathan and Jamel, and my godson, Russell, we arrived at the hotel on August 14, 1989, two days before my son's birthday. Everyone was having the time of their lives. My mom was worse than the kids, in and out of the water, wading and splashing.

As always, I felt proud of being able to provide for my family and give them the things I didn't have growing up. I was happy to take care of my mom and make sure she never had to break her back cleaning white people's houses again. But my heart was troubled. Three weeks before the Disney trip, I had taken a friend to visit her mom in a neighborhood I wasn't familiar with. She didn't have a car, so I offered to help. As the saying goes, "No good deed goes unpunished."

It was so hot that I got out of my car and leaned on

the driver-side door, attempting to feel any part of whatever breeze was blowing. As I stood there, two guys walked up to me and started talking. I recognized one of them. We fist pumped and started talking. I could see he was distracted. He kept looking over my right shoulder, which caused me to turn around to see what he was focused on. Time slowed to a crawl as my mind pieced together the elements of the situation, and I became conscious of what was getting ready to happen: three guys, guns pointed at me, they see me seeing them, they're here for me.

The men were twenty yards away. I surmised that they were hoping their accomplice would have kept me occupied a little longer so they could get closer, but now that I could see them, they started shooting. Every impulse in my body pushed me forward, my brain screaming, "RUN!" I left my car on the street, pushing past the dude I was talking to as he tried to block my path. He was no match for my force. I kept running while bullets flew past my head. Later, I found out that Julio had been nursing a grudge because I fired him as my supplier a year earlier. He waited until I wasn't looking to send some of his goons to take me out. I got away without being shot. The whole situation made me more concerned that something had to give.

I was getting too old and too tired to keep dodging bullets. I have heard so many people who spent their lives as drug dealers talk about how they reached the same point. It's inevitable. You can't live with that heightened sense of paranoia, constantly chasing your money and looking over your shoulder, waiting for the next person who wants to kill you to finally get the job done. You wake up every morning wondering, 'Is this the day all this is going to catch up with me.'

On one hand, I wanted to get out, but on the other hand, I knew there was no way I was going to be able to take care of my family the way I had been with a nine-to-five job. Who was going to hire me and pay me what I was already earning? I was bringing in as much as $12,000 a day. I could not see a way to make a transition from the life I was living to one of peace and still have the things I wanted.

On the morning of August 15, 1989, we woke up ready to enjoy the parks. We were on our way out when the phone rang. I ran back in to answer it and heard Lamont on the other end. He told me that Black had been killed the night before. I was stunned. We had our beef, sure, but I was broken when I got the news that someone had taken his life. My first thoughts were 'who' and then 'why'. How did this happen? I asked Lamont but he said he didn't know. He had just found out himself and didn't know the circumstances. I thought to myself, "Is Julio trying to start some kind of turf war?"

Black's death stirred up so much emotion. I was struggling with my life choices and contemplating who I wanted to be. I had narrowly escaped three gunmen. I had two girlfriends, and it was becoming increasingly difficult to juggle them both. I was tired of my life the way it was, but I didn't know how to change it without losing everything. And now someone in close proximity to me was gunned down. It could have been me. I wondered if I was next.

We stayed at the Quality Inn and ran up a huge phone bill. This was before cell phones when you were charged by the minute for long-distance calls. I had run up an $81.92 phone bill on our first day, and I guess the hotel staff were concerned I might skip out on it. They asked me to come down to the front desk to pay for it. I did and shoved the receipt in my pocket. I had no idea that this receipt would be the linchpin to my case almost twenty-five years later.

I was in Florida with one girlfriend, but my heart was leaning towards the woman I had left behind in Brooklyn. My restlessness made me get up the morning of August 16, 1989 and catch an early morning flight home, even though we weren't due to return home until the following day. I was desperate to see my other girlfriend. I felt all turned around inside with everything that was going on.

That morning I dropped my family off at the park

so they could continue to enjoy the rest of the trip. Johnny, my son, was disappointed, and the girlfriend I had taken with me to Disney World was heartbroken. I was not in the right headspace and hadn't been for some time. I was constantly hurting the people that loved me and promising to make it up. I wasn't the kind of father I wanted to be, the kind of man I envisioned. My life had completely exhausted me, and it was all my own choosing.

I left my car with my Uncle Eddie while I was in Florida. I gave him strict instructions not to let anyone drive except Lamont. Uncle Eddie picked me up from the airport and took me directly to meet my girlfriend who worked as a court stenographer. She and I dropped him off at home and we spent the night at her place as I tried to make up for how I had treated her.

The morning of August 18, 1989, was like any other Brooklyn morning in the Summer. Me and Lamont were on our way to the corner store when I noticed police cars approaching out of the corner of my eye. I thought to myself, "Damn, here we go again." I wasn't concerned that anything was about to go down. I figured they were just going to try to take my money, and since I didn't have much on me that morning anyway, they were going to be disappointed. I kept it moving, but I was caught off-guard when the officers grabbed me and put me in a chokehold. I felt the officer's hot breath as he whispered in my ear, "I'm going to stand right here and slow up your money."

I thought to myself, 'Just take the money.' I was struggling to get out of the officer's grip, but I was prepared to stand down and let them search me. One of the officers drew his gun and told me to be still. There wasn't any use in becoming a statistic that day so I kept it chill. I was thrown to the ground without warning and for no reason that I could discern. They handcuffed me and threw me into the back of the police car. They never said what they were picking me up for but I wasn't worried. This wouldn't be the first time the police wasted my time by arresting me and taking me to the precinct only to release me later for lack of evidence.

When I got to the station and they started questioning me, I realized they were trying to connect me to Black's murder. I was confident because I knew I had not done anything and that there was a bunch of evidence proving it. I waived my rights knowing I was innocent and had a conversation with the detectives.

I was wearing the same jeans I had on when I paid the phone bill at the hotel in Florida. The officers searched me again and found the phone receipt dated and time-stamped for approximately three hours before Black was shot. The office called Florida to verify my story, which checked out. Those Florida officers went to the hotel and were able to get signed affidavits from two of the hotel staff saying that I was in Florida at the time of the murder. The Florida officers sent a letter to the Brooklyn detectives stating the same. That letter was never turned over to my attorneys, so it was never a part of the trial. I found out the letter existed during the investigation that resulted in my exoneration. The detectives knew about the letter before I was indicted but never shared it with the D. A.

They'd kept me waiting in the interrogation room for a long time, but I still had every expectation that I was going to be released. My story was verified, and there was no way I could have been in two places at one time. So imagine my surprise when the officer came back into the room and said, "I got your ass . . . Yeah, I got your ass now Nigger!" and placed me under arrest for the murder of Darryl "Black" Russell. As he read my rights with the satisfaction of a fisherman who just caught a prize-winning fish, I felt like I had left my body. My mind was still not accepting that it was going down like that. They let my girlfriend pick up my belongings. We had both been certain that this could not last long; we were both wrong.

Connie Keys lived in an apartment in the Williamsburg projects. Remember that I hired her so that we could use her apartment as a stash house. Early in the evening of August 14, 1989, the night before Black was shot, Connie was at home watching television when three men, two of whom Connie knew, kicked her door down and demanded that she give them money. The men thought Black had hidden money at her house, and they wanted it. They searched for the money but didn't find what they were looking for. Refusing to leave empty-handed, they stole her microwave. After Black had been shot, Connie easily identified the three men and gave Detective Kenney a full description: a guy with crossed eyes she didn't know but believed was the shooter because she saw him holding the gun, James "Lamont" McCullum (my cousin who I had let use my car), and Joe Samuels.

Black had collapsed near her kitchen window after running to escape his killer, but she thought he had gotten away. She saw him running away from the shots, but she didn't see him fall. She didn't know he had been shot until later the next day. Black and Connie were close. Even though she was fearful that the three guys would come back for her, she told the detective everything she could. Connie's testimony never made it into the trial.

It's a detective's goal to solve a murder within the first forty-eight hours. Detective Kenney had hit the jackpot within that timeframe after Black was killed, but he didn't share his findings with anyone. When he wrote up his formal notes, he purposely omitted any mention of Connie or of the three men. He put my name down as the shooter instead. Connie had given him a full account of what had happened that night, but he conveniently kept that information out of his narrative. None of the three men Connie named were ever suspects in the crime. I became the prime suspect even though I was more than 1,100 miles away at the time Black was gunned down. There is no way I could have committed the crime.

After Detective Kenney interviewed Connie and crafted what seemed like a plan to frame me, he proceeded to line up witnesses to corroborate his concocted version of events.

Jackie was a homeless drug addict, sleeping in the back of a van one of the neighborhood folks allowed her and a friend to use so they wouldn't be on the street. On the morning of August 16, 1989, Jackie was sleeping in the van. Jackie woke up to the sounds of someone banging on the van door and thought it was her friend. As Jackie reached towards the van door to open it, police officers forced the door open. The officers forcefully told her to exit the van. She complied. The police ran the plates and searched the van. The van was stolen, and even though Jackie and her friend were just sleeping in it, they were arrested for grand theft auto.

Jackie was already on probation and had warrants.

She did not want to go back to jail. When she was questioned, in order to avoid more jail time, she told the officer that she could give them information about Black's murder. She told the police she saw me shoot and kill Black and drive away in my car with another man named Cee. This could not have happened since I was in Florida with numerous witnesses at the time the shooting took place.

Jackie told an elaborate story about how Black was arguing with some guys whom she couldn't identify, and then she saw Hook pull out a gun and shoot Black. The detective assured her she would not be arrested or have to testify if she kept talking. The detectives had her look at mugshots, and on cue she picked my picture. She was released after that. Records show she was arrested and charged with auto theft, but her case was dropped that same day.

She was the sole eyewitness and the only person who testified at the grand jury. Her testimony got me indicted. She was apprehensive, but the D.A. told her not to worry because the case would never go to trial. Ten months later, they had to track her down for the trial.

In order for my case to go to trial, Jackie had to go to what is called a Wade hearing, which is an identification hearing. It takes all of five minutes. This is when Jackie would have to formally identify me as the person who committed the murder. She would be asked if she saw the person who killed Black, and she would have to say 'Yes'. That would be the end of the Wade hearing.

But that's is not how it went down, at least not at first. The day we were in court for the Wade hearing was different. When the court officer called Jackie to the stand, the D.A. asked the judge if he could approach the bench. Then he asked the judge to postpone the Wade hearing until the following day because the witness wouldn't testify. Jackie was in the building, but she was refusing to get on the stand and say it was me. The judge asked the D.A., "Do we have a change in testimony?" The prosecutor said 'No', but claimed the witness was afraid of what might happen to her if she identified me since I was a well-known drug dealer. The judge said, "Listen, if you don't have this witness come to identify this man tomorrow morning at the Wade hearing, I'm going to release this man on his own recognizance and possibly dismiss the case." The following day, when we got in the courtroom, my lawyer advised me that Jackie was there and that she was ready to testify against me.

*JACQUELINE BELARDO, a witness called on behalf of the People, after having been first duly sworn, took the witness stand and testified as follows:*

*THE COURTS: Ms. Belardo, would you speak loud enough so that anybody standing right in the back of the courtroom can hear you? Otherwise, you'll have to keep repeating.*

*Louder.*

*Remain quiet, please.*

*All right.*

*DIRECT EXAMINATION BY MR. LEEPER:*

*Q. Directing your attention to August 15, 1989, at approximately 2:15 A.M., in front of the 189 Stagg Walk, were you a witness to a shooting at that time?*

*A. Yes, I was.*

*MR. WALTERS: Your Honor —*

*THE COURT: Yes, counsel?*

*MR. WALTERS: I am going to ask counsel not to lead this witness. I understand it's a preliminary matter, but I think the proper question would be: "Where were you and were you not in front of —"*

THE COURT: Thank you.
*Objection overruled.*

*Q. Did you recognized any of the shooters on that night?*

*MR. WALTERS: Your Honor*

*THE COURT: Sustained*

*Q. Did you recognize anyone at the scene of that shooting?*

*A. Yes. I did.*

*Q. And what were the names?*
*You have to speak up, Ms. Belardo.*
*Did you know the names, or know those people by any names, at the time of shooting?*

*A. Yes.*

*Q. What did you know those people, the names to be?*

*A. As C and Hook.*

*THE COURT: C?*

*THE WITNESS: Yes.*

*THE COURT: Is that C?*

*THE WITNESS: Yes.*

*THE COURT: S-E-A or S-E-E?*

*THE WITNESS: Like the letter C.*

*THE COURT: And Hook?*

*THE WITNESS: Yes.*

*Q. Once again, I just asked you to speak up because we all need to hear. This individual that you recognized as Hook, how long have you known this individual?*

*A. About a year, a year and a half.*

*Q. I'm sorry?*

*A. One year or a year and a half.*

*Q. Did you know Hook's real name?*

*A. Not until later on.*

*Q. What have you learned Hook's real name to be?*

*A. Jonathan Fleming.*

THE COURT: *Please Speak up.*

THE WITNESS: *Jonathan Fleming.*

Q. *Now during that year and a half period of time, can you tell he Court how often you saw Hook?*

A. *About two or three times a week.*

Q. *And where did you see him?*

A. *Between Scholes and Leonard.*

Q. *And where is that located, that intersection?*

A. *In the Williamsburg Project.*

Q. *And when you saw him during that period of time, did you ever talk to Hook?*

A. *Two or three times.*

Q. *Two or three times in total?*

A. *Like once or twice a week.*

Q. *Pardon?*

*A. Like once or twice a week.*

*Q. And what did you talk to Hook about those times that you spoke to hm?*

*A. It was hello and bye.*

*MR. WALTERS: Excuse me? I didn't hear that.*

*THE WITNESS: Hello and bye.*

*THE COURT: Hello and goodbye?*

*THE WITNESS: Yeah.*

*Q. Did you discuss anything else with Hook?*

*A. Just drugs, that's all.*

*THE COURT: Just what?*

*THE WITNESS: Drugs.*

*Q. Well, what was the nature of your conversation with Hook concerning drugs?*

*MR. WALTER: I'm going to object, your Honor.*

*THE COURT: Sustained.*
*Don't answer.*

*MR. LEEPER: Your Honor –*

*THE COURT: The nature of the conversation, Counsel, is not important for this hearing. The extent of the conversation is, the circumstances under which they spoke, but not the nature of the conversation.*

*MR. WALTERS: Additionally, I'm going to ask that A.D.A. Leeper, during the course of this trial, assiduously stay away from that arena.*

*THE COURT: Counselor, I will not make a pre-ruling as to what he may ask or not ask during the course of the trial, depending upon the way the trial develops, and we'll make each ruling on the way it is spoken.*

*MR. WALTERS: Thank you.*

*Q. So how many times did these conversations take place?*

*A. Twice a week.*

*Q. Now, were you ever shown photographs in connection with this case?*

*A. Yes, I was.*

*Q. And do you remember when you were shown photographs in connection with the case?*

*A. A couple of days later.*

*Q. When would that be?*

*A. Sometime after August.*

*Q. And when you say "a couple of days later," a couple of days later from when?*

*A. From the date of the shooting.*

*THE COURT: From when?*

*THE WITNESS: The day of the shooting*

*Q. And what were you shown at that time?*

*A. Some photographs.*

*Q. Who showed you the photographs?*

*A. Some detectives.*

*Q. And when the photographs were shown to you what did the detectives say to you?*

*A. If I recognized any faces.*

*Q. Did you recognize any of those photographs?*

*A. Yes, I did.*

*Q. And who did you recognize in those photographs?*

*A. I recognized Hook.*

*THE COURT: You have to speak louder. Please speak louder.*

*THE WITNESS: I said I recognized Hook.*

*Q. Is that the same "Hook" that you've been referring to?*

*A. Yes.*

*Q. Now, after the shooting, did you ever physically see Hook again?*

*A. Yes, I did.*

*Q. And when was that?*

*A. At the precinct.*

*Q. Pardon me?*

*A. At the precinct?*

*Q. What precinct was that?*

*A. At the 90.*

*Q. You have to speak up. And when was that?*

*A. A couple days after that.*

*Q. A couple days after what?*

*A. After the shooting.*

*THE COURT: After what?*

THE WITNESS: *After the shooting.*

*Q. And what did the – when you saw him, where in the precinct did you see Hook?*

*A. Through a window.*

*Q. And was Hook alone or was he with anyone?*

*A. He was alone.*

*Q. And was he standing or sitting down?*

*A. He was sitting down.*

THE COURT: *He was what?*

THE WITNESS: *Sitting down.*

*Q. Were there police present when you saw Hook?*

*A. Yes.*

*Q. And what did they ask you?*

*A. If I knew who he was.*

*Q. And what did you tell the police at that time?*

*A. That I knew him to be as Hook.*

*Q. Is that the same Hook that you've been referring to?*

*A. Yes.*

*Q. Now I want you to look around the courtroom. Is the individual that you know as Hook, is he here in the courtroom today?*

*A. Yes, he is.*

*Q. Would you please point him out and describe what he's wearing.*

*A. He's wearing the gray suit.*

*Q. Would you please point him out.*

*A. He's sitting over there.*

*THE COURT: Point to him, please.*

*THE WITNESS: (Indicating.)*

*THE COURT: Indicating the defendant, counselor.*

*MR. WALTERS: Yes, your Honor*

*MR. LEEPER: I have no further questions, your Honor.*

It was obvious from her performance on the stand that Jackie did not want to be there. She barely spoke above a whisper which aggravated both the Judge and Leeper. Walters questioned Jackie too. He called into question her ability to see the crime from a football field and a half away without wearing her glasses or contacts.

Jackie confirmed that she did give her story to the police, but that they stopped her on the street, told her they needed her at the precinct, and then made her get into the car with them to be transported to the station. When she got to the precinct, she told the police that she saw me distinctly from that distance. However, she could not tell Walters how I was dressed or whether or not I had on glasses. She also said she identified the car as mine, but she said she wasn't sure it was my car. None of that mattered. She had sat on the stand under oath and pointed to me as the person she saw kill Black. As the only eyewitness, her testimony was the entire basis of the prosecution's case.

For the record, I knew a guy named Cee, but he was a casual acquaintance whom I haven't seen since before I went to Disney World with my family thirty years ago. I never knew his real name. There are no notes in the file that mention that Cee was ever questioned in connection with Black's murder. As far as I know, Cee was never sought out, never brought to trial for having been my accomplice. There was no evidence in the file that we could find noting an interview or even his name, other than in Jackie's testimony. If the police believed Jackie's testimony, why did they neglect to question Cee? It's as though the prosecution completely ignored him in the proceedings. But if what Jackie said was true, even a novice prosecutor should have brought Cee in. After all, he would have been another eyewitness. I still don't know why Cee, like so many other pieces of key evidence, was completely ignored.

Anthony Davis, aka Shawn Diggs, aka Ronnie Diggs, aka Larry Diggs, aka Anthony Shaw, was arrested in February 1990, six months after my arrest. He became a witness for the prosecution in my case then, but neither I nor my attorney found out he was testifying until he was called to the stand during the trial. I heard the district attorney say, "The people would like to call Anthony Davis." No one came to the stand and the bailiff approached the D.A. to tell him that his witness had taken off. The D.A. asked the judge to approach the bench and requested the judge postpone the case until the afternoon.

The D.A. sent the police to go find Anthony; he was hiding out in his neighborhood in East New York. They brought him back to court to take the stand. He was held, just like any other prisoner. When the trial got started up again in the afternoon and Anthony was called to take the stand, he entered the courtroom from the bullpen, but when his testimony was over, he stepped off the stand and went right out the front door a free man.

Witnesses are never held in the bullpen unless they are in custody. If they come from the bullpen, you can safely assume that they are going back to jail once they're done testifying. Theoretically, witnesses cannot be coerced or held in prison until they testify. The D.A. sent police officers to pick up Anthony, bring him back to court, hold him as though he were a prisoner, and made him testify.

Anthony testified that he saw me five minutes before Black was killed and that I had approached him and asked him if he had seen Black. He said 'No'. He then said that I lifted my jacket and showed him the butt of the gun and said: "If you see black tell him I got something for him." Five minutes later, he heard shots and ran to where he thought the shots came from. He saw Black on the ground. It was like watching a scripted episode of Law and Order. Any thinking person had to know he was lying. There is no way in hell anybody living in the projects or casually walking by is going to run towards gunshots. It would never happen.

The real kick in the ass is that he was sworn in under the name of Anthony Davis. He took the stand and swore on the Bible to tell the truth.

"Do you promise to tell the truth, the whole truth, so help you God?"

*"Absolutely, my name is Anthony Davis."*

Every time he got arrested, he would give a different name and a different birth date. Technically, his testimony should have been inadmissible because he was sworn in under a false name. The prosecution was so thirsty to convict me that legal tenets didn't matter. By the way, his real name is Richard Shaw, but no one in the Brooklyn prosecution office thought it was important to check his identity before having him testify.

Yolanda Rossa is another drug addict who said she saw me shoot Black so that she could escape a charge. When it came time for trial, Yolanda refused to testify, saying that she did not want to be forced to lie on me. She never took the stand.

## 4

# JUSTICE DENIED

AFTER MY ARREST, I SPENT TWO DAYS IN JAIL BEFORE I was scheduled to go before the judge. As I waited for the judge, a lady walked up to me, extended her hand and said, "Hi, my name is Ellen Sachs, and I am your court-appointed attorney." I made a fatal error out of the gate by not hiring a private attorney. The reason, like most of my reasons, was money. I didn't want to spend my money on a case that a monkey could have tried and won. There was too much evidence proving my innocence, so I didn't think I needed to pay for an attorney. Plus, I would have to explain where I came up with the money for an attorney. I was still in disbelief, but I was pretty sure there was no way this case would proceed once they heard what I had to say and saw my mountain of proof. In hindsight, I wish I had hired Johnny Cochran, but as they say, hindsight is 20/20.

Ellen told me that because she was a legal aid attorney and not a public defender, she was only able to represent me at the initial hearing. Legal aid attorneys cannot represent clients in murder cases. Before she could finish giving me her speech, I told her I wanted to testify before the Grand Jury. She agreed to add that information to my case file so that anyone taking the time to review the file would know my wishes.

The Grand Jury is made up of everyday people just like a trial jury. Their purpose is to help the prosecution decide if there is enough evidence to take a case to trial. They don't decide whether a person is guilty or innocent. New York grand juries can have as few as sixteen people and as many as twenty-three, while trial juries are limited to twelve jurors. The Grand Jury has more flexibility and can hear evidence that might not make it into the trial. The unique thing about New York grand juries is that defendants can testify in front of the Grand Jury.

New York State Statute §190.50 says you have a right to speak in front of the Grand Jury and to call witnesses. Many black defendants aren't aware that they can testify in front of the Grand Jury, so they miss the opportunity to be heard before an indictment is handed down. The phone bill receipt and witnesses were undeniable proof that I was not a murderer. I knew that if I could get in front of the Grand Jury, I could successfully plead my case. But I never got that chance. The only witness to speak to the Grand Jury was Jackie.

Six days after being charged with Black's murder, the day the Grand Jury had to indict me or release me on my own recognizance or dismiss the case altogether, I got on a bus headed to the courts. I sat in court all day while case after case was called. I was anxiously waiting to meet with my attorney and to get my chance to tell the Grand Jury my story because I was certain they would hear me and know there was no way I could have done this.

My mom, my girlfriend, and my son were each waiting to testify that I was with them in Florida from August 14, 1989, until the morning of August 16, 1989. They would talk about the places we ate, the parks we went to, the fun we had, and even their disappointment when I left on the morning of my son's ninth birthday to head back to New York. There was video footage of our trip, and I appeared in those videos. After hearing all the evidence I had, no sane person could conclude that I was involved in this murder.

Since Ellen Sachs could no longer represent me,

the court appointed what is known as an 18b attorney. An 18b attorney is a private attorney, but he or she is obligated to take a certain number of cases as a public defender. I learned at the end of that day that my new court-appointed attorney was William Lupo. Mr. Lupo never bothered to introduce himself to me or to hear anything I had to say about the case. Apparently, he had another case that day which conflicted with mine, so he gave my case to another attorney, Mr. Joseph Ostrosky. Mr. Ostrosky also didn't think it was important to come to talk to me. At no time in my life have I ever seen, talked to, or had any contact with Attorney Lupo or Attorney Ostrosky.

As the day wore on, I became increasingly restless and agitated. I had chosen not to get an attorney but to allow a public defender to represent me. I expected to talk to my court-appointed attorney before he or she stood before the judge on my behalf. I waited from 10:00 a.m. until 5:00 p.m. and then my name was finally called: "Jonathan Fleming." I'd had all day to prep my speech, and I was ready. The officer came over and I stood up, primed and anxious to tell my story.

But then the officer directed me to get on the bus to go back to jail. I said: "Wait, I am supposed to go before the Grand Jury." The officer was matter-of-fact.

He told me that I wasn't going before the Grand Jury because I had already been indicted.

"What? I didn't even see the judge. I didn't see anybody. I've been sitting here all day waiting for my turn with the Grand Jury." But the officer wasn't hearing me and sharply pushed me towards the van.

My head was swimming. How could this be real? How could I be indicted? I didn't kill Black. I was told that my attorney, Mr. Ostrosky, whom I never even met, had waived my rights without even seeing if that is what I wanted to do. It was documented that I wanted to talk to the Grand Jury. The judge had to see it if he looked at the case, and if Mr. Ostrosky had taken the time to look at the case, he would have seen it too. No one in that court that day followed the law, and I ended up paying for it with a large chunk of my life.

I hired Attorney Robert Walters, a black man who understood the corruption in the Brooklyn police department and D.A.'s office. I thought if anyone could get me off, it was him. He heard my case and put in a §190.50 motion to dismiss the indictment for the ineffective assistance of counsel. Judge Albert Koch, the presiding judge over my case, denied the motion. All he had to do was question the attorneys of record, but Judge Koch also ignored the law in my case and refused to dismiss the indictment or allow me to go to the Grand Jury. The indictment stood as it was.

The A.D.A. at that time was James Leeper. Among his colleagues, who were primarily white, he was respected, even revered, for his ability to win. The problem with his winning record, though, was that it was largely against minority defendants. He wasn't known to be a champion for the truth. He had a reputation for doing everything he could to make sure black men were incarcerated, regardless of guilt or innocence. In Leeper's estimation, if you were black, then you were guilty, and he used the power of the D.A.'s office to lynch as many minority defendants as he could. If the evidence didn't exist, he would make it up. He suppressed and ignored evidence and used his ability to influence juries to weave stories that couldn't be true. Jurors were so mesmerized by his delivery that they ignored the evidence.

My trial began on July 11, 1990. For the entire year I spent in jail waiting for trial, I was certain I was going to get out; my belief was constant. I just needed someone to hear the facts. No one who could make a difference had listened to my side of the story up to that point except Attorney Walters. When Walters got up to speak to the court, he started by stating that he would be presenting a Proof of Alibi defense, which meant he would be presenting evidence that showed I was not in New York at the time of the murder. Then he mentioned that I would be taking the stand in my own defense, but that was a mistake. We had already decided that I would not be taking the stand because doing so would open the door for me to be questioned about my drug dealing. This could make things worse in the jurors' eyes. From the outset, Attorney Walters was in over his head and was taking me down with him.

Unless you have sat through it, your mind can't comprehend what it is like to watch the prosecution parade coerced witness after coerced witness up to the stand to say that you took a man's life. I had no recourse - nothing I could do to save myself - nothing I could say that would jar the prosecution into going after the real killers. The witness's stories were inconsistent, and I wanted to get up and yell to the jury: "Can't you see that none of this could have happened? I didn't do this. The prosecution is willfully coercing these people to lie to you in an effort to build a case that doesn't exist."

I still deal with this today. Some assume that because I dealt drugs that I must have killed people too. I'm not looking for a pardon, but I want to give some people a reality check. Dealing drugs and murder are not one and the same. I have done a lot of things I am not proud of. My list of regrets reads like a dictionary. But, I never crossed over into the darkness you have to fall in to in order to look into a person's eyes and then snuff out their God-given life. I wanted to be able to tell the jury that, but they wouldn't have been able to hear me over the deceit of the prosecution. To them, I was just another black drug dealer who had killed another black drug dealer named Black.

When people tell me that they believe in the justice system, I give them a side-eye. I know right then that that person doesn't know the first thing about how the judicial system actually works. In court, the evidence that later cleared me wasn't being presented, and some of it was never turned over to Attorney Walters. I could have gone home then, but Detective Kenney purposely kept that from happening by withholding several crucial pieces of evidence. The D. A. had to know I was innocent but winning was more important to him than justice for Black.

Over the course of dealing with this ordeal, I learned that there is no such thing as an unbiased person, judge, police office, prosecutor, let alone an unbiased twelve-person jury. A prosecutor is a storyteller that banks on the psychological principles of human behavior to win cases. They call family members of the victim to elicit emotional responses. They call expert witnesses so that the people listening are persuaded into believing that what the prosecutor says must be the details as they occurred on the night in question. Unless you have an attorney equally good at storytelling, which Walters was not, you are at the mercy of how good a story the prosecutor can tell and how much they can manipulate the jury into believing their story. Prosecutors play a shell game with justice. I wasn't a stranger to court proceedings, but this was something out of a movie. From the time of my arrest until the time the verdict came down, I held out hope I would be acquitted. I never had a chance.

Walters came across aloof and sarcastic. I say this with respect because I am not an attorney and I am not familiar enough with how to try a case to tell you everything that was wrong with his approach. He wasn't going to be bullied by the prosecution, but he lacked the skill and insight to circumvent Leeper's blitz.

During Walter's summation, I couldn't tell if the judge didn't enjoy his defense style, didn't like him personally, or if Leeper was just better at prosecuting cases than Walter was at defending them. Walter's close was disjointed and lacked precision in some places. At one point, he said that Jackie gave testimony which she had not given. He then proceeded to tell the jury that it didn't matter because the jury would have the trial transcript and could check the accuracy themselves. Leeper objected during Walter's close seventeen times; sixteen of those objections were sustained.

Walter only objected three times during Leeper's close. The judge overruled Leeper once. Below is the final portion of Walter's closing arguments:

*Now, ladies and gentlemen, I don't know what the A.D.A. is going to say, but whatever he says is going to be with a straight face and, logically, cannot deny that Mr. Fleming was in Florida on the 12<sup>th</sup>, and he flew back to New York on the 16<sup>th</sup>.*

*So, he's got to make you believe that Mr. Fleming snuck up and snuck back. Wow. He has a beef that can't wait until the weekend. He's going to be a frequent flyer and that he's going to fly down on Saturday, and you saw the video. It looks like all day Monday. Then he's going to jump on the plane, I guess at eleven o'clock, eight o'clock, fly to New York, do this homicide with C, and then in the morning run back to Orlando, Florida, and stay there a couple for hours, and then leave the next day.*

*Does he have any evidence of that? Not a shred. Not a shred, because it didn't happen like that. Now, ladies and gentlemen, I'm going to sit down in a couple of moments. I submit to you that there is no way that there cannot be any reasonable doubt in your minds.*

*And again, I'm not asking you to be unreasonable. I gave*

*you reasonable doubt. I gave you airline tickets, I gave you tour packets, I gave you videos, I gave you testimony, I gave you business records, official documents from U.S. Air, from Continental, from the hotel (indicating).*

*It don't get no better than that. If that is not reasonable doubt, ladies and gentlemen, I don't know what is.*

*When we selected you, I asked you to promise me that you will use your common sense and not go off half-baked on some speculator theory that Mr. Fleming is a frequent flyer. Is it possible? Yes. I can't deny that. But is it probable? No. Is it possible that the C.I.A. came to Williamsburg and did it?*

*MR. LEEPER: Objection, your Honor*

*THE COURT: Sustained*

*MR. WALTERS: Possible. But is it probable? No. And on that basis, ladies and gentlemen, I ask you - I don't want to be so presumptuous as to demand of you, the only reasonable verdict that the evidence will allow, and that is a verdict not guilty.*

*How does the record go? I'm not asking for a lot. I laid it out for you. It's not up to me to solve the District*

*Attorney's case. I gave you something to hang your hat on, Capital R, Capital D. Reasonable doubt. I gave you numerous items of reasonable doubt.*

*And even if you don't like my alibi, how could you like that identification?*

*Thank you very much, ladies and gentlemen. And I ask that you return the only verdict that is consistent with common sense, and that is a verdict of not guilty.*

*Thank you.*

After Walter took his seat at the defense table, A.D.A. Leeper stood up and gave the jury a story which he knew was full of lies. He delivered it masterfully and came across as sincere, as though he was seeking the best interest of Black's family and the citizens of New York. All along, though, he was just trying to add another feather to his hat.

*So, ladies and gentlemen, what happened here? Now I'm summing up and I will end it.*

*The defendant was in Florida initially, and many, many calls were made to Brooklyn and the information that was received during those phone calls, and from the testi-*

*mony itself, it would appear, the defendant was making those phone calls, caused him to return to the New York Metropolitan Area on any number of flights (indicating).*

*And what evidence are you going to have? Given that no identification is checked, and given that any name could be used when one boards an airplane and it's never going to be checked or confirmed, how are you going to ever see any evidence of that? And he returns to New York where he is seen by Michelle Moses, he is seen minutes before the shooting by Anthony Davis, and he is seen at the time of the shooting by Jackie Belardo.*

*And prior to the murder, he speaks to Randy Williams and he says 'I'm tired of taking his — taking his shit, and him taking shit from me, and making me look like a sucker, and he has to get his'.*

*And there you have the motive. And that night the defendant and C, an associate of the defendant's, comes out in front of 199 Stagg Walk, and they both pull out guns and they both fire shots at the deceased.*

*And with all those flights, and without any confirmation or using any names, could the defendant have gone back to Florida? Yes.*

*And I submit to you that he did. The 16th. And Black knew there was a problem that night, knew that he was in trouble, because he was trying to get a gun, and they argued, and when he turned his back he shot, and whether the fatal shot is fired from the defendant's gun or from C's gun, it makes no difference, because when you examine it all together, they're acting together with the same intent.*

*They arrive at the scene together, they both point – take out handguns, fire the handguns, and point them at the deceased.*

*And of those shots, it doesn't matter, when you listen to the Judge's instructions, one of those shots strikes Darryl Rush in his back and causes his death.*

*So, ladies and gentlemen, that is the overview of the evidence, and I submit to you that when you take the People's case and the evidence that was produced for you and the conditions that this shooting was observed under, and the witnesses who testified and their absence of motive, I submit to you that that proves this defendant's guilty beyond a reasonable doubt.*

*And that the evidence that was presented by the defense case, under no obligation, but that was presented by the defense, examine very carefully its relevance, and keep your eye on the ball. This is August 15ᵗʰ that we are concerned with, and the events taking place up here in Williamsburg, Brooklyn, and I submit that after you really reflect and consider this evidence objectively, and fairly, and without emotion, you will come to a verdict.*

And with that, my life was in the hands of twelve jurors. Nine days after the trial started on July 20, 1990, the jury sent a message to Judge Koch saying they were unable to reach a unanimous decision. During the jury deliberation, Judge Koch told Leeper and Walters there was a problem with one of the female jurors. She was crying during the deliberations. When that came up, my lawyer believed that maybe she might be the one who thought I wasn't guilty and that the rest of the jurors were trying to change her mind. The pressure was probably too much. I can only speculate, but I think she may have been the juror that saw through the smoke and believed in my innocence.

Judge Koch called all the jurors out to let them know that he'd heard there was a problem. He advised them to go back into the jury room to see if they could agree on a verdict. It was Friday. If they didn't come back with a verdict, they would have been sequestered through the weekend. The jurors went back into deliberations and returned around 2:40 p.m. with a verdict. I felt the earth move when the foreman said: "We, the jury, find the defendant guilty." My ears felt like they were filling with water, like I was being swallowed in the ocean, unable to swim to safety. The sounds in the courtroom became muffled as I sat in disbelief, struggling to come to grips with what I had just heard.

Through all the noise that was vibrating outside of me and inside of me, I could make out the sound of my mother howling through tears: "No, no, no, no". My supporters were crying and trying to understand, just like I was, what universe we had just walked into. One of my aunts fainted. People yelled and hollered out that what the jurors had done was wrong.

*"He could not have done this. He was in Florida."*

*"How did you come back with that verdict?"*

The jurors were terrified and asked to be escorted out of a back exit and to their various cars. The reality that I would not be going home set in with a vengeance. I kept wondering how the jurors could see the videos from our trip to Florida and think I could have been anywhere near Brooklyn on the night the crime was committed.

Somehow, Leeper had bewitched twelve thinking, breathing, human beings into believing that it was possible for me to be at the hotel desk in Orlando Florida at 9:30 p.m. on the evening of August 14, 1989 paying a phone bill, and then to leave the hotel, drive to the Orlando airport, catch a flight from Orlando to Newark under a fictitious name, pick up my car, drive an hour from the Newark airport to the Williamsburg Projects in Jersey, shoot Black at approximately 2:00 a.m. on the morning of August 15, 1989, get back in my car, drive another hour back to the airport, catch a 3:00 a.m. or 4:00 a.m. flight under a fictitious name back to Orlando, Florida, and then drive back to the hotel all in time for breakfast at the Quality Inn on the morning of August 15, 1989. Then I dropped my family off at the park and got back on a plane to Newark on the morning of August 16, 1989. IMPOSSIBLE!

But like I said, the jurors could not hear the truth over the prosecution's fraud because they had already made up their minds. That is the only thing that makes sense.

Within two weeks of my conviction, Jackie recanted her testimony. She had run into my mom, and my mom begged her to tell the truth. My mom said Jackie broke down in tears and told her what the police and the D.A. did to her. After hearing her story, my mom asked her if she would be willing to tell the story to my attorney. She agreed. She called my attorney that same day and went to see him the next day. She was pregnant, and her water broke while she was at the attorney's office, but she refused to let her boyfriend take her to the hospital until she had finished her affidavit.

*I, Jacqueline Belardo, writing this the way I saw it on August 15, 1989, and I swear this is the truth. I was hanging out with a friend of mine in a Debbie Amar building on the second floor and saw a friend of mine get shot behind his head. I was in front of the window smoking a cigarette. All I saw that night was to my instinct was Hook's boys and two guys arguing with Black. It was dark, but not dark enough to see that Black got shot in the head with two bullets. It was too far and a little dark for me to recognize the faces or even their bodies. I ran down after the shooting towards where Black's body fell and saw him laying there. Where everybody ran to, I don't know. But I am here writing this because I know it wasn't Hook or Cee that shot Black because I made them up. Because a couple of days later, I was arrested in a stolen van and was scared plus I violated probation and I had a warrant. So made them up when asked about who shot Black. The detective said if I have seen anything or know anything, I could be released that same day. Judge, I am not being threatened or paid off. Just I've been in a drug program and I have my focus on myself and mistake and God knows I made a terrible one for lying. Plus the detective said I would never appear in court which next thing you know I was subpoenaed. Which also, I had a drug substance in my system which was crack cocaine. So I went through knowing I was wrong. Just didn't know how to get out of it. Then one year later, which I thought was my dark nightmare. No one would ever know that I lied but myself. They found me. The homicide detective in June 1990 brought me in for questioning and I told them I wasn't sure of what I saw but he said I could never change my story because what I said at the Grand Jury. They also said I could be held for perjury. So they made me very nervous, and I felt a lot of pressure. And I even wanted to take a polygraph so they could see I wasn't sure. I could not recognize them from that distance, plus I was high too. I felt I had to do it their way. But I did it wrong again. Now they made me lie at the testimony on trial. God, I felt like shit, too scared. I didn't know who to trust. But I came to realize since I testified, I can't sleep knowing I lied. Going to my recovery clinic and in our encounter groups, I told them my wrongdoing. Just didn't know how to relieve these wrongdoings, so this is why I write this. I am free from a lie, and I ask you to please understand the situation I was in.*

Because Jackie recanted her testimony, my attorney filed a motion to set aside the verdict before sentencing based on newly discovered evidence. I was supposed to be sentenced on August 10, 1990, but instead of being sentenced that day, the judge granted a hearing on the motion to set aside the verdict. We had witnesses lined up.

Jackie came into the courtroom rolling her new baby in a stroller. She left the baby with my mom while she gave her testimony. She told the judge she didn't see me kill anybody. The judge asked her why she testified the way she did at the Wade hearing that I was the killer. She told the judge that she was pregnant at the time. On the day the Wade hearing was scheduled to take place, she was in the D.A.'s office refusing to testify. She did not want to be the reason I went to jail. She said the D.A. left her in his office while he came into the court and asked for the continuance. After the judge granted the continuance, the D.A. came back and told her that if she didn't get on the stand the following day and say I was the killer, that she would be put in jail, forced to have her baby in prison. Again, the D.A. held her in his office, going over questions and giving her the answers they wanted her to repeat until well after midnight. When they were done grilling her, they took her home and then came right back early that same morning to transport her to court for the second Wade hearing.

She told the judge she could not live with the nightmare of knowing that she had sent me to prison on a lie and that she had given the testimony the way she did because she had made a deal with the district attorney to drop the theft and drug charges against her in exchange for her false testimony against me.

Tony Jimenez, nicknamed Germ, testified that he had given the gun to Lamont, Joe, and the crossed-eyed shooter. He also said he witnessed the murder but was not involved.

Jerry "Mailbox" McGee was addicted to crack. He testified that when I was in Florida, Lamont had run out of product and had McGee take him to another supplier to buy enough product until I got back. Jerry said when they were on the way back, he was sitting in the backseat with Rose while Lamont and Joe were in the front seat. He was across the courtyard in the archway and saw Rose shoot Black.

Michael Bennett testified that he heard the shots fired and saw Lamont, Joe, and another guy he didn't know jump in my car and drive away. He did not see me at the scene.

The judge listened to all the testimony and then took about two weeks to come back with a decision on the hearing. For that entire two weeks, I was on cloud nine. After all that testimony, there was no way I was going to prison. I gave away everything I kept in prison to other inmates because I knew I was going home. When the judge started to give his decision, I was dazed. He did not believe the witnesses. He said he thought that Jackie had been telling the truth during the trial but had lied during the motion hearing. He told her that she was now a perjurer, but she was never charged with perjury. He believed she only changed her testimony because she was afraid of me. He then gave his sentence, twenty-five years to life. I was flattened, and I had to get all my stuff back from the other inmates.

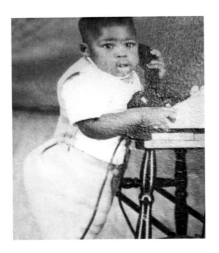

This is me as a baby. Who knew my life would
take so many twist and turns.

Inmate 78699557868868868

My mom bringing my sons, Jamel and
Jonathan to visit me in prison.

**City of Orlando**

100 SOUTH HUGHEY AVENUE
ORLANDO, FLORIDA
32802-0913

TELEPHONE
(407) 849-2470

October 16, 1989

New York Police Department
90th Precinct
211 Union Avenue, Room 246
Brooklyn, New York

Attention: Detectives George Kenney
and Jim Devereaux

Re: Case #1291
Suspect: Jonathan Fleming

Investigator Morman has obtained the following information
in response to your request concerning Mr. Jonathan Fleming's
visit to Orlando in August, 1989.

Investigator Morman met with Mr. A. Dennis Corrado, Director
of Security, Quality Inn, 7600 International Drive, Orlando,
Florida, on August 28, 1989, at 1315 hours. Mr. Corrado
provided Investigator Morman a copy of the Room Registrations
for rooms 1457 and 1459. The registration covers August 12
through August 17. A copy is enclosed. Mr. Corrado also
provided a copy of the Telephone Record for room 1457, which is
enclosed for you.

Investigator Morman met with the Hotel Housekeeping Staff
and learned that different individuals cleaned rooms 1457 and
1459 each day between August 12, and August 17.

    August 12 - Housekeeper - Madeleine Bertres
    August 13 - Housekeeper - Rosa Monta
    August 14 - Housekeeper - Anita Berber
    August 15 - Housekeeper - Rosa Peres
    August 16 - Housekeeper - Dennis Baptiste
    August 17 - Housekeeper - Rosa Lee Sinclair

Letter from the Orlando police following their investigation
which proved I was in Orlando at the time of Black's
murder.

Investigator Morman has contacted these persons and showed them photographs of Jonathan Fleming. No one made a positive identification. This hotel has approximately 57,000 guests per month.

On August 28, 1989, at 1335 Hours, Investigator Morman spoke with Gloria P. Lloyd, B/F, DOB: 5/14/58, a front desk clerk at the hotel. Ms. Lloyd identified the photographs of Jonathan Fleming and stated that she recognized him as checking into the hotel, but does not recall seeing him again. (Check-in time is usually at 1500 Hours.)

On August 28, 1989, at 1430 Hours, Investigator Morman interviewed the front desk cashier, Renee Robitaille, W/F, DOB: 7/3/69. She identified the photographs of Mr. Jonathan Fleming. She stated that she recalled him, as he had been wearing a lot of gold jewelry at the time he checked into the hotel on the afternoon of August 12, 1989. She remembered the family due to their large telephone bill. She further states that his mother paid the phone bill and stated that she was checking out the next day. She recalled that the woman stated that her son had left that morning. She paid the telephone bill at approximately 1900 Hours of August 16.

I hope this information is of benefit to your investigation. If we can be of additional assistance, please contact us.

Sincerely,

T. R. Scoggins, Lieutenant
Violent Crimes Section

TRS/ea
Enclosures

```
     QUALITY INN
     ORLANDO, FL     .
-----------------------
     ROOM 1457-2      .
-----------------------
CASH          81.92-

AUG.14'89 09:27PM
320360 01 AUG 13 .
```

Phone bill receipt from the Orlando hotel proving I was not in New York on August 14, 1989. It was found in Detective Kenney's files.

*Homicide 1989.*

*VICTIM: "Black" Darrel*

*Notes from Detective Kenney written before my arrest identifying Black's murderer and his accomplices.*

Attorney Anthony Mayol.

Investigators Kim Aklin and Bob Rahn.

After being exonerated, the first thing I wanted
to do was hug my mom.

Me and mom outside the courthouse.

Me with District Attorney Kenneth Thompson.

R.I.P. Eugene Boney

Vaughn, Kenny, me

Front right to left: Johnny (grandson) ,
Jonathan (son), me, Jamel (son), Darius (son).

I share my story with as many people as I can to educate
them on the epidemic of wrongful convictions.

Being interviewed on Fox News

My mom was my lifeline and even though I miss her everyday, now I live those days to make her proud.

5

# THE WORLD TOUR

I HAD DONE TIME BEFORE IN MINIMUM-SECURITY prison, but it's a whole different mentality when you are locked up in a maximum-security prison. You're doing time with the worst of the worst, guys who murdered, guys who raped, and guys who molested children. These guys don't have anything to lose. I saw young men get raped and couldn't do a thing about it. I saw grown men cry like babies. Committing any infraction could get you more time, but some of these guys were doing fifty years to life, or one hundred years to life, or five consecutive life sentences. What was another couple of years? They didn't have any hope of ever getting out, so they lived their lives like they were never getting out. When there is no hope of living, then life becomes about dying. It's like an undercurrent of death wishes coursing through the veins of prisoners in maximum-security facilities.

I cannot tell you I did my time like a champ, or I took one for the team, or I was a model prisoner. Quite the opposite. How do you serve a damn near life sentence like a champ? Especially when you are aware of your innocence with every breath you take? I'm a different man now, but back then I was not in a good head or heart space. I was angry; I was bitter, and I was still trying to be the Hook of the projects. I got into fights with inmates and guards. I stabbed an inmate, and I was stabbed by an inmate. I sold drugs and schemed in every way I could to survive and to not be in prison poverty. I still had to hustle to take care of my family, so I set up shop in prison.

Prisoners are creative because they have to be. You have to come up with ways to have normal everyday things when those things aren't available. Say you want to play chess but you're locked up in solitary; then you have to make a chessboard and chess pieces. You take a legal envelope, draw a checkerboard on it, and write in the numbers in each square. Then you tear off pieces of paper and make your pawns, rooks, queens, and kings. If you want a drink, there are inmates who can make liquor. If you want to talk on the phone, there is a way to get your hands on a cell phone. If you want something particular to eat, it might be difficult to come by and you might have to sell your soul to get it, but in prison, where there is a will there is a way. With creativity and coercion, you can get pretty much anything you want, or at least a decent substitute for it. If you wanted to get high, then I was your guy.

I made prison work for me in the ways that I could. The food in prison is something that isn't even fit for an animal, but I figured out how to have a decent meal from time to time. At the beginning of the month, I would check the schedule to see what was on the menu. I would see what days they were serving chicken breast or fried chicken, and then I would barter with people to get their ration. This way, I could end up with four or five chicken breast or eight pieces of fried chicken at one time.

There isn't much to do in prison, so you read or "get your swole on." You find ways to get your body as fit as possible. It's really the best kind of fitness because you are using your body to create the resistance that builds muscle and makes you lean. The prisons are full of people that look like Dwayne Johnson or Arnold Schwarzenegger in his day. I think it's a part of human nature to have plans and set goals. When you are serving long or indefinite sentences, you need to set goals so that you stay sane. Goals give you something to look forward to, something to strive for. Fitness is one of the few things an inmate can control, even when they're in solitary confinement.

The depression, anxiety, and mental illness inmates suffer is real, but there is no one who cares enough to help them cope with those issues. You can be prescribed meds, but the confinement makes the illness worse. I watched a man tie a bedsheet to the crank normally used to open a window and then tie the other end around his neck. I still hadn't figured out what he was doing when he started running away from the window at top speed. He purposely killed himself in one of the most horrendous ways I've ever witnessed rather than wake up another day in a cage. I once held a man's legs while guards untied him from the pole in the shower after he decided prison life was too much for him. He regretted surviving.

Did I consider taking my life? Yes. I'd wager that most inmates do at one time or another. A man can lose his mind in prison, but I thought about what that would mean for my family; my mom who agonized over my wrongful incarceration as much as I did; my sons who were having their own struggles and legal battles; all of the people who believed in my innocence. I was facing life in prison, but I still had reasons to live.

I was never the kind of man that picked a fight, but I never ran from one, either. I carried myself every day just like I had in Williamsburg and Marcy. I made myself valuable, and that is how I survived. From the time I was convicted in 1990 until 2012, I was the prison drug dealer. I never got caught with drugs. I did get caught conspiring to smuggle when one of the ladies who brought in drugs got busted and her boyfriend singled me out.

I spent nearly a third of my time in prison in solitary confinement, or the box, as we called it. The box is a 6x8 cell where I spent twenty-three hours of every day alone. I've seen men lose their grip on reality in the box. Sometimes, there was a cell door, and sometimes there was a metal door with a window that had a slot where the guards could pass my food to me. Nobody came to see me or talk to me, so I had to improvise. I would talk to people through the cracks of the door, or I would lay on the floor and push my face up against the door to talk to whoever was listening through the small space between the door and the floor. I was in a cell that was next to a cell that was next to another cell. I couldn't see the people in the adjacent cells, and they couldn't see me, but we each could see the cement wall across from our cells.

I could see people as I passed them by when the guards came to take me from my cell for a shower. I got three showers a week, one every other day. When it was time for my shower, I stood in front of the cell door with my back facing the door while leaning over so that the guard could put handcuffs on me through the slot where I normally got my food. The guard would put cuffs on me and order me to stand up straight and walk towards the wall so that he could enter my cell while keeping an eye on me. I had to stay in that standing position facing the wall until the guard told me it was okay for me to move. When the guard gave the order, I would back out of the cell slowly as the guard directed me to the shower.

The shower was a box too, the size of regular stand-up shower but with cell bars. I had all of seven minutes to bathe and shave. The shower was on a timer and it was common for inmates to exit the shower covered in soap because they weren't fast enough. There was a sink in my cell but I swear it was designed to avoid giving up hot water.

I carried myself with bravado because a maximum-security prison is the last place you can show even the slightest sign of weakness. I also didn't run around talking about how innocent I was. Doing so would be like extending an open invitation to have everyone try me to elevate their prison status. I had to make it known that I had no problem handling business if business needed to be handled. This got me in trouble quite a bit, and I racked up a lot of frequent flier miles in the box.

What people don't know about being in prison is

that it is rare that a prisoner will serve all their time in one prison. If you get an infraction and have to go to the box, when your time in the box is up, you are moved to another prison. I traveled all over New York from prison to prison, like I was on a twenty-five-year state-wide tour. I stopped by all the most popular prisons in the state.

- Downstate Correctional Facility – Oct 1990 to Dec 1990: This is a reception facility. Prisoners stay here for up to sixty days while they are classified as minimum, medium, or maximum security. Once they are classified, they are assigned to the appropriate facility and transferred out. I was only here long enough to find out where my next stop would be.

- Elmira Correctional Facility – Maximum – Dec 1990 to Sept 1992: I swapped with another inmate to stay close to home.

- Shawangunk Correctional Facility – Supermax – Sept 1992 to 1996: During my time at Shawangunk, I went to the box twice. The first time I spent six months because of a dirty urine sample. The second time I was given eighteen months for assaulting a staff. Two days after I was released from the box for the assault, I was transferred from Shawangunk to Attica.

- Attica Correctional Facility – Maximum – 1996 to 1997: Attica is its own kind of hell and could easily have its own chapter in this book. It is the Guantanamo Bay of prisons. The guards are far more dangerous than any inmate ever thought about being. Some of them have a black baby with a noose around its neck tattooed on their arms. This let me know they were looking to hurt blacks. I was informed on my first day there that I would be killed if I caused any trouble. I made the mistake of talking in line on the way to chow my first day, and the guard singled me out and talked to me like I wasn't a man. There is no dignity in prison, but I'm still human. It was another guard who saved me. He looked at me from across the room and motioned to me by moving his head back and forth as if to say "No." He was letting me know that that if I chose to say anything back to this guard, who was yelling at me and spitting in my face, that that guard was prepared to fix it so that I was never able to speak again. The guards were known for brutality. They were sadistic animals, turned loose on prisoners with no expectation to respect human rights or any other type of rights. I went to the box for sixty days and went back to population. It's the only time I was released from the box and not immediately transferred. I'm not sure why I was eventually transferred from Attica, but I welcomed the transfer.

- Clinton Correctional Facility – Maximum – 1997 to 1998: I got eighteen months in the box for extortion and I was transferred to Southport box facility to do the eighteen months. I was selling drugs and a man who owed me money, paid me by having his family send the money to a friend of mine on the outside. The inmate then reported to the warden that I was extorting money from him. This was a common practice in prison. If an inmate was threatened or just wanted to get back at you, they might give false information to the warden or guards. This information would usually result in you being removed from population. I originally received eighteen months in the box for the extortion, but I appealed it and they reduced my box time to one year. I put in for a reconsideration and then they dismissed the charges altogether. It was considered a wrongful conviction coincidentally, so I received a check for a couple hundred dollars for the eight months I was in the box without cause.

- Southport Correctional Facility – Maximum – 1998 to 1999: This was primarily a box facility meaning nearly all the inmates assigned to this facility were doing box time. I received a year in the box but served nine months with time off for good behavior. I'm not sure what I did that time to end up in the box.

- Elmira Correctional Facility – Maximum – 1999 to 2001: There was a gang war between the Crips and the Bloods. I wasn't gang-affiliated, but I was selling drugs and the guards felt I had influence over what was happening. They even asked me to talk to the gangs to see if I could stop the war, but I told them I couldn't get involved. The last thing an inmate needs to be caught doing is advocating for the prison authorities. I wasn't planning to spend the rest of my life in prison, but I had to maintain my reputation for the time I was there. I was transferred to Comstock. This time I wasn't the only one being moved. There were other prisoners thought to be influential who were unwilling to ruin their reputations too. We were all transferred out to different facilities as punishment for our silence.

- Comstock Correctional Facility – Maximum – 2001 to 2003: I stayed in involuntary protective custody for nineteen months after a prisoner who owed me money for drugs wrote a letter to the superintendent saying I was going to get stabbed in the yard that night. There was no real threat. This was another example of a fearful inmate making up a story to have me removed from population. I was in the box at Comstock on 9/11 when I received the news about the World Trade Center.

- Green Haven Correctional Facility – Maximum – 2003: I spent three months in the box for sending cash money in the mail. It is against the law for inmates to send any type of currency in the mail.

- Auburn Correctional Facility – Maximum – 2004 to 2005: I received one-year box time for conspiring to smuggle narcotics. They transferred me to Upstate Correctional Facility to do my box time.

- Upstate Correctional Facility Maximum – 2005 to 2006: Upstate is another box facility. I was only here for a year to serve my box time for the conspiracy charge.

- Clinton Annex – Maximum B – 2006 to 2007: I requested a transfer to this facility to be closer to home.

- Eastern Correctional Facility – Maximum – 2007 to 2008: I received two years box time. My girlfriend at the time got caught trying to bring me heroin and marijuana into the facility. She was sentenced to three years.

- Southport Correctional Facility –
Maximum – 2008 to 2010: I was sent here
a second time to serve by time in the box.

- Coxsackie Correctional Facility –
Maximum B – 2010 to 2011: The same girl
who brought me drugs before, brought me
more drugs. This time she put the drugs in
a potato chips bag. I passed the bag to
another inmate. When that inmate was
being transported back to his cell, they
checked him and found the drugs. He told
them I had given him the drugs. I got a year
of box time, which I served at Green
Correctional Facility.

- Green Correctional Facility – Maximum –
2011: I was given a year in the box, but
only served eight months due to good
behavior.This was not my only time at
Green, and it wasn't because I liked the
accommodations.

- McGregor Correctional Facility – Middle –
2011: I was given ninety days in the box for
being accused of inappropriately touching
my girlfriend on a visit. This was a straight-

out lie. I imagine the guard didn't like me and that's why he did it. He never mentioned the inappropriate touching to me during the visit, nor did he try to stop the visit. The next day I got a ticket with the charge. I called my girlfriend and told her what happened. She said she was going to file a complaint. I told her that when I saw the guard, I was going to say something to him. They must have been listening to my call because within twenty minutes of getting off the phone call, they were at my cell handcuffing me to take me to the box. After I got out of the box, I was transferred out of the facility.

- Washington Correctional Facility – Medium – 2011: This was a medical facility. I got a ticket but the ticket was later dismissed and I was sent to Wende.

- Green Correctional Facility – Medium – 2012: This was my second time at Green. This time I served ninety days of box time for fighting. After I served the ninety days, they sent me back to Wende.

- Wende Correctional Facility – Maximum – 2012 to April 8, 2014: I was released from Wende.

The days passed slowly and the years stretched on while the people that meant the most to me went on without me. My mother was the love of my life. From the time I was born until the time she died, she never let me want for anything. Her pain was real. I was her only child, the son she had always wanted, and we were apart. I took care of her in every way I could, but without me helping her, she had to go back to cleaning people's houses.

Mama was NaNa to the neighborhood. Everyone loved her. If you didn't have a place to sleep, you could crash on her couch. She suffered most when I was convicted. My sentence was her sentence too. I didn't fully understand her pain until my son was sent to prison for taking a man's life.

My mom came to visit me and my son was supposed to visit with her, but when I came into the visitation room, I didn't see Johnny. The look on my mother's face told me something was wrong. I will still upbeat as I walked up to her. I asked her where Johnny was. She looked at me and said: "Johnny is in jail." She began to cry, and I felt my stomach drop. I wanted to know what was going on with Johnny, but the concern in her voice made me almost too afraid to ask. I sat across from her and asked, "For what?" She said, "For killing somebody." All the wind was sucked out of me. How could my child be in jail for murder? It broke my heart.

I have four sons; I didn't know Vaughn existed until he was seventeen. The first time we met in person, he was thirty-two. His mother kept him a secret until her aunt died. Her aunt and my mother lived in the same project. When she came for her aunt's funeral, she told my mother about Vaughn. He was conceived when she was visiting one summer.

It's normal for a boy to aspire to be like his father, to want to grow up and be a fireman or a police officer. I didn't give them anything to look up to when I was out of prison and being in prison kept me from being there for them. I know that the life I led for so many years impacted them negatively and was one of the reasons they got into trouble. They didn't know anything else because I wasn't there to show them a better way.

When I went to prison, Jonathan was nine and Jamel was five. Darius was conceived while I was in prison. I missed every milestone, every birthday, every holiday. Jamel was a popular basketball player with a chance to go to college and maybe even the NBA, but that never happened. I always wonder how differently my sons' lives would be if I had been a different kind of father. Would they have gone on to be engineers? Airline pilots? Doctors? Lawyers? What could they have become if I had modeled that for them? To this day, no matter how much I've changed, and no matter how much I pour into my sons, they still choose to live their lives doing some of the things I used to do. It bothers me more than anything, but I hold on to the hope that one day they'll get it.

I got married three times in prison. Prison was miserable and I needed hope from the outside to come to me regularly. I welcomed marriage, whether I thought it was right or wrong because I didn't want to be alone. I did love the women I married with the capacity I had to love at the time, and I went in to every marriage with the thought that it would last. Marriage gave me hope that something could be good when nothing really was. In prison, marriage is something to look forward to and celebrate in a place where there is no reason to do either. Most marriages between inmates and people outside of prison are doomed from the onset, but that doesn't stop people from trying it.

New York allows conjugal visits for married inmates. Inmates sign up for these visits, which could be as often as every six weeks if you pick weekdays, and up to every three months if you sign up for a weekend. At the time of your visit, you are given access to a trailer on the prison grounds. It's like an apartment, far better than a cell where you can spend two days with your wife. You have to lean out the door during inmate counts so that you can be counted, but other than that, you have a weekend alone with your spouse, with no interruptions. As long as you're in good standing, you can partake in these visits. Given my recurring visits to the box, I missed a lot of these visits, but I had my share.

My whole time in prison was about me trying to maintain hope and make a living. I didn't know how to live differently. Everything I had been exposed to set me up for a life in prison. Even though I was there for something I didn't do, dealing drugs put me on the path to be in prison one way or another. I hadn't come to accept that then. I was still trying to be Hook.

6

# A THEORY

I'VE TRIED TO UNDERSTAND WHAT TOOK PLACE THAT night in 1989 when Black was killed. There are so many bits and pieces of information that I've quilted together over time. I'm not sure if anyone will ever know the entire truth. It's certain that at least one of the men who killed Black got away with murder, and although the other two people were identified and one of them has confessed, the other one died in a car accident. I'm not sure the Brooklyn police department will ever bring charges against the real killers. No doubt there are many more things that we don't know about what really took place. I could be completely wrong, but based on the information I have and the conversations I've had over thirty years, this is what I think happened:

I planned my trip to Florida for my son's ninth birthday, and I needed to leave someone to manage things while I was away. I left my cousin Lamont in charge of running the business. He was eighteen or nineteen at the time, but I thought he could handle things for four days. My Uncle Eddie kept my car, but I told him that Lamont could use the car if he needed to.

Lamont hung out with Joe, who was around Lamont's age, and who also worked for me. It's apparent now that neither of them was ready to manage work like that, even for a short period. I am not sure if Lamont knew that I had fired Black. I do know that he brought Black in to help him move the product while I was away without my knowledge. I am not sure if Black took the product, took the money, or took both, but I learned from Connie that Lamont came looking for money. Lamont was pissed off and tried to fight Black, but Black was a better fighter and embarrassed Lamont.

Lamont then got his high school friend Rose involved to help him get back at Black. I don't know if they planned to kill him, or if things got out of hand and they took it too far. The way I understand it, they were in a frenzy looking for Black, and they knew Connie and Black were close. When they went to the apartment looking for Black and neither he nor the money was there, they became even angrier. While the guys were in the apartment, Connie was in another room talking to Black through the window. She told him how Lamont, Joe, and Rose came into her apartment looking for him and took her microwave when they couldn't find what they were looking for. She was upset, and Black told that it would be okay; he would buy her another microwave.

Lamont, Joe, and Rose heard her talking to Black and realized that Black was outside the window. They ran out of the apartment around to the window, and that's when Connie saw Rose point the gun at Black. Black took off running, but they shot him in the head. Connie said she didn't see the shots. She only saw Black running, so she thought he had gotten away and was okay. Obviously, he wasn't. He was running, but he only got a little farther away before he collapsed from the shots.

Lamont, Joe, and Rose jumped into my car and drove to Joe's house where Bernice, Joe's sister, overheard them talking about the murder. Everybody went home, and Lamont went back to pick up my car from Joe's house the next morning. Bernice was with him. and the two of them dropped my car off to my uncle. My Uncle Eddie picked me up from the airport the next morning; he didn't know what had happened the night before. Connie went to see Detective Kenney to tell him her story before I came back from Florida, but he must've already decided to make me the responsible party.

Lamont is the one who called me the morning of August 15, 1989 to tell me that Black had been killed. He acted just as shocked the rest of us. Lamont came to visit me for the first few months I was in prison, but he never said anything about knowing what happened or being involved.

I had been in prison for about eight years, and I had spent all that time trying to figure out the sequence of events that landed me in prison. I had written letters to anyone I could think of who might be able to do something with my case. Many people told me if I could provide adequate compensation, that they would help me. I had one attorney tell me that he couldn't help me and refused to return my calls. After I was released from prison, that same attorney reached out to my attorneys and pledged his commitment to help them work on my case. I treated him the same way he treated me and refused to return his calls.

I was talking with my mom one day when she told me Bernice Samuels wanted to talk with me about something. Bernice was Joe Samuels' sister. Joe was one of the men Connie Key said was present when Black was killed. My mom helped me get in touch with her. When she first got on the phone, we had a minute of small talk, but then she told me that Joe had died in a car accident a few months earlier. I told her I was sorry for her loss. Then she said: "I have some other information I want to talk to you about, but I know you are going to be upset with me. It's concerning what you are locked up for."

She told me the day that Black got killed, Lamont, Joe, and a guy named Rose parked my car in front of her house. The three of them went upstairs to talk about the murder. Based on what she heard, she said Rose was the one who had done the shooting. They were all scared. Lamont left my car at her house all night and walked home. He came back the next morning and took the car back to my Uncle Eddie. She said she was with him when he took the car back. She told me the reason she hadn't come forth before then was because her brother was involved and her family told her to stay out of it. She also said that her brother told her that if my cousin would come forward, that he would come forward too. I asked her if she would be willing to talk to an investigator and she said 'Yes'. But it wasn't until after 2013 that she finally did it. Every time someone tried to talk to her, she said she was scared. She believed Ross had killed before, and nobody really knew how bad of a man he really was. She was afraid he would come for her.

I read Connie's report in the case files during the

trial, so I kind of suspected that Lamont was involved in some way. I even asked him while referencing Connie's report, but he swore he never had anything to do with it. When I first went to prison, Lamont used to visit me and put money on my books. This man whom I trusted looked me in my face, knowing how I was suffering, and never once admitted what he had done. It would take until November 2013, before he finally sat down with Bob Rahn and Kim Anklin, the investigators I hired on April 8, 2013.

Lamont's affidavit is what prompted the D.A. to revisit my case. Four days after Lamont's interview, I was called to court to sit down with the Brooklyn Integrity Unit. That's when they told me what they had discovered in Detective Kenney's case file. There was a letter from the Orland Florida detectives confirming they had spoken with two hotel staff that testified I was there in the hotel at the time Black was killed. That letter was never turned over to the defense at trial. Neither was the phone receipt that they took out of my pocket during the search at the precinct when I was interrogated.

I guess now it doesn't matter what happened, except that I still believe someone should be brought to justice for killing Black. Maybe the powers that be feel the time I served was enough, but I think Black's family would disagree. In 2018, in pursuit of further damages for the time I served, my attorneys laid out the facts of the case like this:

## Factual Background

*On Tuesday, August 15, 1989, at approximately 2:15 AM, the victim, Darryl Rush Alston was tragically shot in front of 199 Stagg Walk, Brooklyn, New York, at an apartment complex located inside the Williamsburg Housing Projects. Mr. Alston was taken to Woodhull Hospital where he later died.*

*At the time of the fatal shot was fired in the early morning hours of August 15, 1989, Mr. Fleming was in Orlando, Florida with his family, having been there from August 12, 1989 until August 16, 1989. There exists no credible evidence to the contrary.*

*On August 18, 1989, after he had returned from vacation in Florida, Mr. Fleming was arrested in New York for the murder of Darryl Rush Alston. At the time of Mr. Fleming's arrest, he had in his pocket, a time stamped receipt proving that he was in Orlando, Florida paying a hotel phone bill at 9:27PM on the evening of August 14, 1989, making it physically impossible for him to have been at the site of the murder of Darryl Rush Alston which was alleged to have occurred at 2:15AM in the early morning hours of August 15, 1989 in the Williamsburg section of Brooklyn.*

## Belardo – A False Eyewitness

*A few days before Mr. Fleming's arrest in 1989, the New York City Police had arrested a woman named Jacqueline Belardo. Ms. Belardo, at the time an admitted crack addict, had been found by police officers in a stolen van and was in violation of her probation. Ms. Belardo lived in the same housing complex where the shooting of Darryl Rush Alston had taken place a few days earlier. Under intense police pressure and threats, Ms. Belardo, not wanting to face her own criminal charges, fabricated a story that Mr. Fleming (a man she knew from the neighborhood) committed the murder, in order to avoid charges in her own pending criminal matters.*

*Once Ms. Belardo falsely named Mr. Fleming as the shooter, he became a person of interest, despite the fact that he was in Orlando, Florida at the time of the murder.*

*Shortly after Ms. Belardo falsely named Jonathan as the culprit, he was arrested for the Alston murder. When arrested, Jonathan immediately explained to police officers and detectives that he had been in Orlando, Florida with his family on vacation during the time of Darryl Rush Alston's shooting. Jonathan was able to provide photographs, family home movies, plane tickets, and his family members to demonstrate that he was thousands of miles away from New York at the time of the Brooklyn homicide. However, despite providing police detectives with substantial information confirming his alibi, NYPD detectives and the King's County District Attorney's Office insisted on proceeding with Jonathan's arrest and prosecution. Jonathan made no inculpatory statements, and no physical or forensic evidence has ever connected him to the crime.*

*At the time of Jonathan's arrest, police removed his personal belongings, including a time stamped hotel phone bill receipt proving that he was in Orlando, Florida at a time four hours before the Brooklyn murder, demonstrating that he could not have been the shooter. This piece of exculpatory evidence would have demonstrated that Jonathan's alibi defense was credible, placing him over 1,000 miles away from the scene of the Alston shooting in Brooklyn.*

## Belardo attempts to recant her false statements

*Before Mr. Fleming's trial in 1990, Ms. Belardo attempted to recant her false statements against him. By this time, she was seven months pregnant and off of narcotics. Ms. Belardo recalls that members of the New York City Police Department and District Attorney's office threatened her before Mr. Fleming's trial that she would have her baby in jail if she did not testify in accordance with her original statements, naming Mr. Fleming as the shooter. See her affidavit annexed hereto.*

*Under enormous pressure and pregnant, Ms. Belardo testified at Mr. Fleming's trial that on August 15, 1989, she was in a second-floor hallway of 163 Ten Eck Walk in the Williamsburg Housing project, near a second-floor hallway window looking out over the courtyard. She falsely claimed that she was able to see*

*Jonathan at approximately 2:15am during the morning of the shooting from over 400 feet away, in a dimly lit area, with a view obstructed by trees, foliage, a playground, while she was not wearing her prescription glasses for nearsightedness, and while she was under the influence of narcotics.*

*Ms. Belardo has since recanted her statements, coming forward and admitting under oath that she was incentivized to give statements involving the murder of Darryl Rush Alston in order to avoid charges in her own pending criminal matters, and in fact could not identify claimant as the shooter as she originally testified.*

*In addition, even if Ms. Belardo had not recanted, it would have been a physical impossibility for her to have identified Jonathan as the shooter from her claimed vantage point.*

*Ms. Belardo testified that she viewed the shooting through a window located on the 2nd floor landing of 163 Ten Eck Walk. The window is partially obscured by large horizontal and vertical metal bars which obstruct a clear exterior view of the expansive, heavily foliated courtyards below. This diagonal line of sight was measured to be a distance of over 400 feet from the vantage point of Ms. Belardo's window at 163 Ten Eck Walk to the scene of the shooting located at 199 Stagg Walk. A photograph was taken showing Ms. Belardo's vantage point on the 2nd floor landing under the best possible conditions, in broad daylight, replicated by a camera lens of 35 mm lens to replicate what the human eye would be able to see from the second-floor landing. This photograph was taken with the*

130

camera pushed through the metal bars in order to have an unobstructed view.

Of course, Ms. Belardo's view unlike that of the camera,
would have been obstructed by the depicted window slats. To
recreate Ms. Belardo's vantage point and provide the referenced
photographs, demonstrative evidence expert and professional
photographer, Robert Frein, who has over twenty years of demonstrative evidence experience, examined portions of original trial
testimony and went with his associates to the exact location of
Ms. Belardo's alleged vantage point (as she testified to) on the
second-floor landing of 163 Ten Eck Walk. Mr. Frein then had
two of his associates stand where the shooting allegedly took place
outside of 199 Stagg Walk in order to take photographs with a
35mm camera lens to replicate what the witness would be able to
see from the given vantage point.

Because of the tree foliage and the playground in the way,
Mr. Frein was unable to clearly see his associates through his
camera lens. To obtain photographs of what subjects would look
like out of the subject second floor window, he had his associates
step approximately 20 feet to the east and approximately 20 feet
to the north, closer to his vantage point in order to obtain an
unobstructed view. The photograph outlined where the subjects
would have been where the shooting took place, if they were
standing in an unobstructed line of sight, however, the subject
location is obstructed by the trees, playground, and foliage as
depicted. Mr. Frein's associates can be seen to the left, however, as
can be viewed from the photograph, even under the best possible

131

*conditions, taken in broad daylight, it is impossible to accurately distinguish the facial features his two associates, even with an unobstructed view, given distance of over 410 feet away. Ms. Belardo claimed to have been able to identify the Claimant as the shooter in the dark early morning hours at 2:15am, under the influence of narcotics, while she was not wearing her prescription glasses for nearsightedness.*

*The diagrams and photos demonstrate that it would have been impossible for Ms. Belardo to have identified Jonathan as the shooter from her vantage point, as she previously claimed.*

*Demonstrative evidence produced at trial will show that even under the best possible conditions such as in broad daylight, it is impossible to accurately distinguish facial features from Ms. Belardo's claimed vantage point, over 400 feet from the murder scene. Even more ludicrous is the claim that such an identification could have been made on a particularly dark August night around 2:15am, when the shooting Mr. Ashton actually occurred. Finally, and of critical importance, Ms. Belardo admitted during claimant's trial and in affidavits that she was not wearing her prescription glasses for nearsightedness at the time of her alleged observation and identification.*

*In opposition to claimant's motion for summary judgment, the defendant attacked claimant's demonstrative evidence expert, Robert Frein as unqualified to opine about Ms. Belardo's vantage point to the scene of the murder, and unqualified to opine about the visual acuity of the human eye. Claimant has recently exchanged the report of Dr. Paul Michel, an optometrist and law enforcement expert in human vision, and eyewitness identification forensics, who has reviewed the trial testimony, photographs, diagrams, and measurements at the scene. Dr. Michel has similarly concluded that Ms. Belardo could not have made valid or reliable eyewitness identification from her vantage point under the conditions that existed during Darryl Rush Alston's murder.*

## Conclusions of Dr. Paul Michel regarding Impossibility of Belardo Trial Testimony

*In opposition to claimant's motion for summary judgment, the defendant objected to claimant's the qualifications of Claimant's demonstrative evidence expert, Robert Frein to opine about the visual acuity of the human eye. Claimant has recently exchanged the report of Paul Michel, OD, an expert in human vision and eyewitness identification forensics who is well qualified in the field and will be testifying along with Mr. Frein at trial.*

*Dr. Michel is an optometrist and former specialist investigator with the Los Angeles Police Department. His expertise in eyewitness identification forensics regarding human vision has been developed and enhanced with over twenty years of experience providing eyewitness identification analysis. Dr. Michel has been qualified in numerous jurisdictions nationally and has provided a scientific assessment of eyewitness identification forensics in both criminal and civil cases. Dr. Michel's analysis provides a scientific assessment of what an individual could or could not discern in various conditions pertaining to vision; these conditions might be affected by lighting levels, distance, movement, time constrains, refractive conditions, eye disease, and other variables.*

*Dr. Michel has reviewed the trial testimony, photographs, diagrams, and measurements related to this case, and like Robert Frien has similarly concluded that Ms. Belardo could not have made a valid or reliable eyewitness identification from her vantage point under the conditions that existed at the time of Darryl Rush Alston's murder.*

*Specifically, Dr. Michel has made the following observations about Ms. Belardo's eyewitness identification from her vantage point:*

1. *The distance between Ms. Belardo and the crime scene was beyond the range that reliable eyewitness identification could occur. Under the best daylight conditions and standard corrected vision, eyewitness identification is not possible at distances much beyond 40 feet. The distance between Ms. Belardo and the site of the shooting was 400 feet or greater. The further the observer is from the scene, the scene appears proportionately smaller. The long distance between the observer and the observed produces:" a relative distance minification". The Visual resolution of any facial identifiable features is impossible even at a fraction of this distance.*

2. *On August 15, 1989 at 2:15 AM in New York City, the sun had been set since 7:56 PM on the*

*previous day. The moon was low in the western sky, less than two hours before setting behind the western horizon. Since Ms. Belardo's line of sight to the crime scene was to the southeast, there would have been no significant natural lighting elements at the crime scene. Since vision is the sensory modality of light, the darkness at this crime scene precludes seeing detail from any distance much beyond twenty feet. Since suspect movement and limited observation time are unknown, they are not factored into the previous opinion. If suspect movements were rapid and observation time was limited, the validity of eyewitness observations would be limited to an even a shorter distance than twenty feet.*

3. *Since vision is the sensory perception of light; vision is dependent upon the intensity of light entering the witness's eyes. Light dissipates over distance, according to "The inverse square law". Specifically, as the distance from the light increased, the intensity of the light diminished as a function of the mathematical square of the distance; i.e. Intensity =1/distance squared. Whatever light fell on the crime scene, would have dramatically dissipated after traveling the distance to Ms. Belardo's vantage point. The distance from the crime scene to Ms. Belardo was in excess of 400 feet. The light at Ms. Belardo's distance would have been much less*

than 1% of what would have been present 1 foot from the crime scene.

4. Ms. Belardo reported having been an illicit narcotics user at the time of her observation of the crime. Visual functioning deficits occur under the influence of narcotics. She was significantly mentally impaired during her reported witnessing of the crime. The observations of the murder scene that Ms. Belardo claimed to have made while under the influence of narcotics, particularly in light of the distance and lighting issues noted above would be categorically unreliable.

5. Ms. Belardo required prescription eyeglasses for clear vision. She was not wearing her prescription eyeglasses when the crime occurred. It is highly probable; she was significantly visually impaired, due to uncorrected refractive error, when the crime occurred.

## Jonathan Fleming's Arrest & the Withholding of Exculpatory Evidence

Jonathan, despite providing substantial information including video supplied by family members establishing his presence in Orlando Florida during the general time period of the murder, could not produce the more definitive time stamped receipt confirming his alibi as it was deliberately suppressed by NYPD *investigating detectives. Police and prosecutors ignored defense requests refusing to produce this critical document until almost 24 years after Jonathan's wrongful conviction. On July 20, 1990, Claimant was wrongfully convicted of second-degree murder, and on November 30, 1990 he was sentenced to twenty-five years to life in prison. Over the years of his incarceration, Jonathan attempted to overturn his conviction with appeals and petitions but was unsuccessful. Over the years, Jonathan hired various private investigators to reinvestigate his case, with no success.*

*It was only in 2013, when Jonathan's family accumulated sufficient funds to retain new private investigators to thoroughly reinvestigate the facts and circumstances of Jonathan's wrongful incarceration that led to the discovery of new evidence and the real murderer. They had never lost faith in Jonathan's innocence.*

*Jonathan's new private investigators interviewed over two hundred witnesses and developed new leads and evidence which convinced the Brooklyn District Attorney's Office to open a full reinvestigation into Claimant's case.*

## The Kings County District Attorney's Conviction Integrity Unit Discovers Startling New Evidence

*In the fall of 2013, the Brooklyn District Attorney's Conviction Integrity Unit revealed that their office had discovered two critical pieces of evidence that were hidden within the law enforcement files for over twenty-three years and had never been* turned over to Jonathan's defense counsel before, during, or after trial. The documents included a time stamped hotel phone bill receipt Jonathan corroborating Jonathan's claim he was in Orlando, Florida approximately four hours before the time of the Ashton's Brooklyn murder and an Orlando Police Department letter confirming that there were independent Orlando witnesses who could confirm Jonathan's vacation to Orlando, Florida during the critical time period in August of 1989.

These two pieces of highly critical information finally disclosed by the D.A.'s Office 23 years after Jonathan's trial were instrumental in bringing about his exoneration. This exculpatory information, hidden within the files of New York City Police Detectives for over 23 years could not have been produced at trial by the defendant, even with the exercise of due diligence by Jonathan or his defense counsel.

On April 8, 2014, after a comprehensive reinvestigation of the Fleming Case, the People joined Jonathan's defense counsel's motion to vacate his conviction under CPL Section 440.10 on grounds of newly discovered evidence, evidence which was hidden for over two decades. In light of the foregoing new evidence, Jonathan, was exonerated on April 8, 2014 by the Honorable Matthew D'Emic after spending twenty-four years, seven months, and twenty days incarcerated for a murder that he did not commit.

The late District Attorney, Kenneth Thompson, released a press statement on April 8, 2014, announcing the dismissal of charges against Claimant. The release quotes then District Attorney Kenneth P. Thompson as follows (emphasis added):

"Today's actions follow a careful and thorough review of the case, and based on key alibi facts that place Fleming in Florida at the time of the murder, I have decided to dismiss all charges against him."

As District Attorney Thompson concluded, Fleming was innocent of the Rush homicide, having been in Florida at the time the actual shooting occurred in Williamsburg. Mr. Fleming spent 24 years and 7 months of his life in maximum-security prisons across the State of New York for a crime he did not commit. His children grew up without a father. He suffered incredibly during this time, spending almost a decade in solitary confinement for often false and trivial prison life offenses. The abuse of human rights caused by the years of solitary confinement Mr. Fleming endured as an innocent man exacerbated his personal suffering in a manner rarely seen in Wrongful Conviction and Civil Rights Litigation anywhere in the United States.

---

7

---

# F-R-E-E-D-O-M

---

PRISON CHANGES YOU, BUT IT ALSO CHANGES THE people who love you. When I first went in, people were calling and coming to visit, trying to encourage me, but after a short while, their visits became less and less. Before long, I was not being visited by anyone but my mom, my sons, and my girlfriend. All the people I had helped and tried to look out for didn't think twice about me. I felt like I didn't have anything but my anger to keep me company.

I never gave up hope of being released, but I got tired many days. There is no way to count the number of letters I wrote and attorneys I begged to take my case. My family exhausted money looking for someone to just take a look at my case files, believing that once anyone read it, they would know I was innocent.

In 1992, my son Jamel's mother, Crystal, was pushed in front of a subway train by a friend of her former abusive boyfriend who was incarcerated for assaulting her. For several days, no one knew where she was, but everyone knew she had to be in trouble because she would never have left Jamel alone. Jamel was only eight years old at the time.

The family looked for Crystal in all the normal places and finally found her listed in the hospital in a coma under the name Jane Doe. She survived, but she lost a leg and several fingers. The damage from the train was irreparable, but she fought as hard as she could. She filed a lawsuit against the transit authority due to the rate of speed the conductor was going. She won the lawsuit in 2005, the same year she died as a result of her injuries from the accident.

By 2005, I had been in prison for sixteen years. Crystal always believed in me, and she wanted to help me get out of prison. I was devastated that she was gone and grieved for my son who didn't have his mother or his father to help guide him. Jamel has always been kind-hearted and he wanted to help me get out of prison just as much as his mother did. When he received the settlement money from Crystal's case in 2012, he gave me money to hire new investigators for my case.

On April 8, 2013, I started working with Bob Rahn

and Kim Anklin. Rahn was an ex-cop, and I didn't trust him at first. I had hired another investigator who was a cop, Les Wolff. He promised to handle my case, but it turns out he was a close friend of Detective Faye, one of the detectives who worked to fabricate evidence in my case. Wolff told me that he and Detective Faye were friends but he still agreed to take my case.

Initially, he was all about helping me, but after he went to an annual 4th of July picnic which he told me was taking place, he stopped taking my calls and answering my letters. Detective Faye was supposed to attend the same picnic. Since Les abandoned my case altogether, I can assume he and Detective Faye talked at the picnic. Whatever they talked about was powerful enough for Les Wolff to forget I existed. There was so much corruption in the New York police department that I didn't believe a former New York police officer was capable of doing the right thing. Bob and Kim convinced me they would do their best to get me out of jail. I paid their fee and they got to work.

I had been in prison for close to twenty-five years and the time for me to go to the parole board for the first time was approaching. It's no secret that when you sit in front of the parole board, they want to hear about how sorry you are for what you've done and how your time in prison has made you a better person. The parole board is not interested in your innocence and standing before them professing your innocence is the best way to get your parole denied. I was adamant that no matter what, I was not going to pretend to be repentant for a murder I was not responsible for. It was important to me that my freedom was granted to me because my innocence had been recognized by the courts.

As a parolee, I would have to wear the badge of guilt, even though I wasn't guilty. I was not prepared to do that. My mom begged me to do whatever I needed to do to get home, but it was enough that I had spent all that time in prison. I thought that acting sorry in front of the parole board would be setting me up for another kind of prison. How many people want to hire someone who has a felony murder on their record? Where does a paroled murderer live? What landlord runs a background check and says "Yes" to the person who has killed someone? I knew that if I lied to the parole board, I was going to spend whatever was left of my life like I had spent the last twenty-four years, with the foot of the New York judicial system on my neck. I'd rather take my chances with Bob and Kim.

As they went through the case file, they were appalled at how mishandled my case had been. They contacted many attorneys to share their findings and asked for their assistance, but after receiving a lot of

"NO's," they went straight to the Conviction Integrity Unit. And that's when things took a turn in my favor.

I had written to D.A. Charles Hynes every year from 1990 to 2013, the entire time he held that office. He originally started the Brooklyn Integrity Unit but he didn't do anything with it. The unit did review my case and discovered the phone bill payment receipt that the detectives had taken out of my pocket the day they arrested me and a letter from two Orlando detectives confirming that I was in Florida the night of the murder. I should have been released five months earlier, following this discovery but D.A. Charles Hynes did not take action. He left the work to the next D.A.

In November of 2013, Charles Haynes lost the election to Kenneth Thompson. I didn't know D. A. Thompson would change the tide of my case when he was elected, but he turned out to be one of the people most instrumental in dismissing my case.

While I sat in prison waiting impatiently for the ordeal to be over, Bob and Kim worked with Attorney Anthony Mayol. Mayol was the brother of an inmate I met in prison. They brought me to Rikers and met with me to let me see the new evidence found by the Brooklyn Integrity Unit. In all that time, I had not cried about what had been done to me, but when I saw that receipt and that letter, I broke down. I wasn't crying tears of resentment; I was crying tears of pure joy. For the first time in almost twenty-five years, I knew that I had been heard, that someone who had the power to free me knew the truth, I'M INNOCENT! And because they now knew it, I was going home.

Kenneth Thompson was the game-changing type of attorney rarely found in the judicial system. One of the first things he did when he took office was start cleaning up the marred reputation of the Brooklyn's D.A., seen as racist and sometimes outright criminal in how it handled cases. He disbanded the integrity unit Haynes started and created an entirely new one.

Within three months of being in office, he dismissed the charges against me and gave me my freedom. He brought my case to the forefront and used it as an example of how much change was needed in Brooklyn.

*In fewer than three years in office, Thompson built his Conviction Review Unit into one of the country's best, focusing not on DNA cases but on decades-old killings that relied less on forensic testing and more on old-fashioned investigative work: reading through old records, re-interviewing witnesses, looking for slip-ups or outright misconduct.*

*Thompson inherited the Conviction Review Unit (CRU) from Charles Hynes, who'd led the office for more than*

two decades and left under suspicion that he'd overseen a
wave of negligent prosecutions.

Thompson, who campaigned as a reformer, took as his
model a conviction integrity unit in Dallas led by a
public defender. That successful unit focused on old
DNA cases. Thompson went further, turning to cases
from New York's most violent era, the 1980s and
1990s — when drug-related killings overwhelmed
authorities, who cleared many cases with single witnesses
and obtained confessions from unaccompanied juveniles.

As Thompson's unit, led by Sullivan, began examining
those cases, a bunch stood out as deeply flawed. The
investigators uncovered evidence that undermined convictions of defendants who'd been sitting in prison for
decades.

In his first year in office, Thompson's unit exonerated 10
people who'd been wrongly convicted of murder. In
2015, they freed another seven innocent people, six of
whom had been convicted of murder. And in the first
eight months of 2016, the unit cleared six more,
including three convicted of murder.

Thompson showed that it's possible for prosecutors,
without changing the nature of their office and without

*giving up other responsibilities, to take the problem of
convicting innocent people seriously and to devote energy
and personnel and commitment to it in a way that makes
a major difference," (NBC News, Oct. 11, 2016.)*

Exactly one year to the day after I hired Bob and
Kim, I was released: April 8, 2014. Two and a half
years after my release, Kenneth Thompson passed
away after a short battle with cancer. He had been an
advocate for me when most people had grown tired of
hearing my pleas of innocence. He even spoke at my
mother's funeral. He was a true American hero, and
his short tenure in the district attorney's office changed
the Brooklyn judicial process.

There are no words that have ever been spoken
that can describe what it was like for me to hear the
judge say, "Your case is dismissed." Imagine being on a
rollercoaster, as it creeps to the top of the first hill, and
then sitting at the top before the anticipated drop.
Then imagine the car you're in plunging into the drop
and the feeling in the pit of your stomach as you
throttle towards the bottom. Now, imagine that you
stay in that drop for almost twenty-five years with that
same feeling in your gut. At first, you are in shock that
anything could be that terrible, but then you settle in
and learn to live in the drop. Finally, someone steps in
and helps you get through the rest of the ride. You

can't believe it when the ride stops, and you are allowed to get off. Your nightmare is over, but your legs are wobbly, and you're unsure of yourself. What are you supposed to do after you get off the ride?

In prison, I learned to live in the drop. My life was a downward spiral into hell, and I became accustomed to it. For twenty-four years, seven months, and twenty days, other adults told me what to do. I didn't have the liberty or responsibility of making my own decisions. All my meals, showers, and bathroom breaks were determined by another person's whim. I talked to people when I was allowed to and kept to myself when I was told to do so. No one expected me to balance a checkbook, pay a bill, go to the grocery store, or find a job that would provide me with enough income to make a living.

The state of New York stole my life and then they threw me out the door after keeping me in a cage without any knowledge of how to survive. No one was there to help me deal with the trauma of having been locked up that long, or to teach me how to navigate all the new things I would experience. When I was released, they sent me through those gates with $93 in my pocket. What was $93 going to do for me in a place like New York?

I'm not complaining now, and I wasn't complaining then. I knew it was going to be a hard road, but I wasn't prepared for how hard. I thank God to this day for my family and my friends who stuck by me. They helped me learn to live again and to thrive.

The feeling of being lost without many options when I left prison is the reason I started the Jonathan Fleming Foundation. I want to be able to help other people in my situation by giving them a good start, something I didn't have when I was released. If I can provide housing, job training, jobs, and therapy services for men and women who find themselves booted out of prison after a wrongful conviction without any support systems, then I can help save these people from being forgotten about and falling through the cracks.

There are other ways you change in prison that I didn't realize until I got out of prison. I found myself way behind the times. I'm still trying to catch up six years later. After my first dinner to celebrate my release, I went into the bathroom at the restaurant and couldn't figure out how to flush the urinal or wash my hands. I couldn't believe it when the toilet flushed by itself. I stood at the sink for a minute trying to figure out how to turn on the water to wash my hands. After standing there for a while, unable to figure it out, I did something you never do as a guy; I asked the man standing next to me.

*"Hey man, how do you turn this water on? I don't see a knob."*

*He laughed and said, "Where have you been?"*

*"I was in prison, man, for a crime I didn't commit."*

He congratulated me on being released and showed me how the water worked. I couldn't believe I was waving my hands in front of the sink to turn the water on.

The first time I went shopping, I was overwhelmed. As I walked with my family on Jamaica Avenue in Queens, I started to feel claustrophobic. There were so many people moving around and talking and doing too many things at one time. My body felt like I was absorbing all that movement into my skin. The sounds of all the voices joined together landed on me like a roaring wave. I became so nervous at one point that I had to stop and stand against the building with my arms stretched out next to me as though I was holding on to the building to keep from flying away. I felt like if I didn't stop and brace myself, I was going to lose something I couldn't get back. We had to cut the shopping trip short.

Then there's the figuring out where you fit. Prison life is a redundant train of sameness every day. I got older, but it was hard to grow or expand my mind. I read books, but the darkness in prison stunts your growth. When I got out, I found that almost everyone had moved on in some way, but I was still in the same place as I had been twenty-five years earlier.

I went to prison as the father of little boys but came back to grown men who had their own families. At fifty-one, it was hard to start parenting thirty plus-year-old men when I had missed some of the most important times of their lives. Even now, the guilt of not being there makes it hard for me to give them advice. I often don't feel like I have a right to say certain things to them, or I'm concerned that they don't value what I say because of where I've been. I see so much of myself in them and I know I have the experience and wisdom to help them, but having been in prison so long seems to invalidate my words.

What you don't find out sometimes until it's too late is that not everyone wants to help you, even when they beg to help you. The news media was following me around. People wanted to tell my story, and there were those coattail riders who latched on to any available part of me, looking to get a piece of the action for themselves. They pretended to care about me, but they were just looking to score from me. I didn't know that at the time.

I went from having nothing to being exposed to everything. I was so happy to be free that I ignored many of the warning signs. After I received my settlement, I paid $60,000 dollars to take thirty of my so-called closest friends on a cruise. I have heard from five of those people since. Everything done in the dark comes to the light, and so before long, I realized that there are very few people I can trust. I don't say that with any hatred. It's just a truth that I live with that makes my life simpler.

One thing was consistent every single day of my prison sentence, and that's the love from my mother. She fought harder for me than anyone else. I was more than happy, beyond excited at being able to hug my mom. It was the first thing I did after they dismissed the charges against me. To be able to hold her in my arms as a free man was the best feeling I'd had in a long time.

Mom was and is my angel. Just like when I was a kid, when I was finally released, all I wanted to do was take care of her, make her life easier, and give her back the time she lost waiting on me to get out of prison. I didn't know as I held her in the courtroom on April 8, 2014, that I only had a little more than a year left to spend with her.

Mom was forty-eight when I went to prison and seventy-two by the time I was released. In those nearly twenty-five years, her health deteriorated. She was diagnosed with diabetes and had to take insulin to control it. Over time, her diabetes affected her kidneys, and she had to go on dialysis. Three days a week for three to four hours at a time, she was connected to a machine that took the blood out of her body to clean it and then put it back in. The dialysis took a toll on her.

When we knew that I would be getting money from the city as compensation for my false incarceration, I promised mom the world. I wanted to get her out of the projects, but at seventy-two, she was grumpy and stuck in her ways. She all but refused to leave Marcy. I told her that when I got the money, she would become a target in the projects. Someone might kidnap her to extort money from me. She loved me more than anything and would not let anyone use her to harm me, so this was the only way I could get her to agree.

I had grand plans for her. The sky was the limit. Whatever Patsy Fleming wanted from me she could have. She could have two of everything as far as I was concerned. I needed to show her how thankful I was for all her love and support all those years. She could not come to see me in prison frequently, but I talked to her almost every day for all those years. She was so much of the reason I did not go completely crazy in the box. Thinking about how she talked, her candor and her fervor for life, her kindheartedness, and how much she loved me kept me going.

In January 2015, nine months after I came home, mom had a heart attack that was so severe it left her unable to walk. She was in the hospital for months before they sent her to a rehab facility. That didn't keep her from being feisty. She was just as demanding as ever, especially to the people at the rehab. I didn't care. I went to see her every day. I was just happy to have her, to be able to take care of her. Even though I didn't have much then because my settlement had not come through yet, I gave her everything I could. She was my girl.

One hot morning in June, mom called me to ask if I would bring her cheesecake from her favorite place, Junior's Restaurant on Flatbush Avenue in Brooklyn. Of course, I was going to get her cheesecake and anything else she wanted. All she had to do was ask. That is the last time I spoke with my mother. I stopped to pick up her cheesecake and headed to the rehab, but as I was on my way, my mom had another heart attack. It was more severe than the last one. She stopped breathing for eight minutes. They were able to resuscitate her, but she was brain dead, and there was nothing I could do. The doctor told me she was gone, but I wasn't ready to take her off life support.

Despite the doctor's prognosis, I still hoped she would wake up. How was I supposed to pull the plug on the most important person in my life? I was in the middle of settling my lawsuit, and while mom was on life support, everything was finalized. I wasn't going to get to shower her with gifts or take her on trips or just sit at the table with her and have a cup of coffee. She was not going to fight me on every little decision anymore or give in because her whole life was about making me happy.

I was still going to sit with her every day, even though she couldn't talk to me. I heard somewhere that even when people are in a coma, they can still hear you, so I talked to her like I always did. I told her the city settled, and I made sure it was a decent offer. She always told me she wanted to see me do it big, so I told her that I would make her proud doing big things to help others. I wanted her to know how grateful I was to her for so much love, and I needed her to know that it was okay for her to go because she had held me up through everything. It was time for her to rest.

I gave the okay to remove her from life support on June 23, 2015, the same day I settled my case. But I told you, Patricia Ann Fleming was feisty. She lasted without life support for another ten days although she never woke up. On July 3, 2015, my angel got her wings. My heart was in pieces. I just got her back, and now I had to let her go.

My mom was never a religious woman, so I was not exposed to church or the Bible. I went to church maybe five times as a child because my aunt made me go. Throughout my time in prison, people kept telling me to trust God and pray and give it to God. My response to them was: "What kind of God would put me in here for a crime I didn't commit and then leave me to die? I don't want to serve that kind of God."

When I was transferred to Auburn prison, I ended up on the same unit with one of the guys from the neighborhood. His name was Natural. I knew of him from the streets. He had his own crew and I had mine. We weren't necessarily friends, but we weren't enemies either. In prison, people from the same neighborhoods stuck together when possible, so Natural and I developed a friendship that remains to this day. He was in to the church and constantly tried to get me to go with him. He told me that only God could help me make peace with my life and deal with the resentment I felt inside. I was not going to be one of those guys who went to church in prison because there was nothing else to do and get 'all religious.' I needed to keep my edge and continue to nurse my hate. I did everything I could to go against God. I wasn't trying to be rebellious. I just didn't know another way, and I was so full of rage that I couldn't see anything else.

In 2012, I was not at Auburn anymore, but I could still hear Natural's voice trying to convince me to try God. I went to church out of desperation. After twenty-one years, I didn't have anything left to lose. To be truthful, I don't remember the content of the message that day. I know I found myself being moved by the words and feeling like someone had told the preacher my story so he made me the subject of his sermon that day. By the time his message was over, I couldn't help but get out of my seat and go to the front of the church. I gave my life to God that day. Even as I write this, I am aware that it was God reaching down for me because He had to know I was not coming to Him on my own.

Natural was released and deported to Trinidad. He was brought here by his parents when he was five years old and knew nothing about Trinidad, but God has favored him there and he is doing well, still helping people to find their way to God.

After I gave my life to God, I wanted to be a different person. I was different. I don't know how saying "Yes" that one day made me over but it did. I gave up drug-dealing and many of the other negative things I did in prison. Something else began to happen, too. The momentum on my case increased. In 2012, my son received the settlement from his mother's accident, and in 2012 and 2013, he gave me money to pay the investigators.

In 2013, Bob and Kim agreed to investigate my case and then they convinced Kenneth Thompson that my case needed another look. Things were moving faster than they ever had. I hung on into 2014 when those pieces of evidence that could have freed me in

1989 were found in the case file. They gave the D.A. no choice but to let me go. All those years, I lived out of my anger, but when I made a choice to let the anger go, God set me free. I was released from prison less than two years after I gave my life to God; that is no coincidence. I was like Paul, fighting against God with everything inside of me, but when I gave up the fight, He gave me my life back.

I've been asked repeatedly if I'm angry at Detective Kenney who set me up, Jackie Belardo who lied on me, Lamont who is responsible for Black's murder but let me take the rap for it, Attorneys Lupo and Ostrosky who didn't think enough of me to even introduce themselves, at the judge who violated my rights by refusing to let me speak before the grand jury, at A.D.A. Leeper for conniving to have me imprisoned, at the twelve jurors who were too jaded to believe me. My answer is 'No'. I was vengeful for a long time but not anymore because I've chosen not to be. If God has forgiven me for so much, how can I refuse to forgive others? I learned the hard way that anger is a waste of time. There is freedom in forgiveness.

I had the chance to speak with Jackie after my release. I was at my attorneys' office being prepped for my lawsuit against the state. Jackie was there giving another affidavit confirming what she had said twenty-four years earlier, that she had lied on the stand when she said I killed Black. When she found out I was there, she didn't want to see me for fear that I resented her.

When I walked into the room where she was sitting, her back was to me, and I could see that she was weeping. I approached her and touched her shoulder. She looked up at me, her face wet and her eyes full of tears as she began to apologize. She didn't even know I was still in prison until the attorneys contacted her to come in for another affidavit. I told her to stand up. Her guilt was obvious as she laid her head on my chest and cried for all the trouble she felt she had caused me. I wanted her to know freedom that day in the way that I had come to know it. I told her: "Jackie, I forgive you, and you can forgive yourself."

I have been able to talk to Lamont since my release. Our conversations aren't long, and I sense that he wants to know where I am as it relates to what he did. He had the power to give me my freedom, but who is to say that anyone would have believed him? There was already so much evidence pointing to my innocence that the D.A. ignored. Or who's to say that the D.A. wouldn't have taken Lamont's story and found another way to weave me into it. He had already made up a story so what's a few more false details?

I went to a family union, hoping to see Lamont. I told my cousin, his mother, that I forgive him and I just wanted the chance to look him in the face and tell him.

I can't say that I would have come forward to tell the truth knowing I would face prison. Lamont did what most people his age would have done; kept his mouth shut. I just need him to know that I don't hold him hostage to his sin and he doesn't have to either.

Being bitter was a way of life for me for way too long. In all that time, it was only God who kept me from being swallowed up by my own frustration. He only allowed so much to come to me. Even those years in the box were God's way of keeping me safe. I can see that now. I didn't need saving from the people who I felt had done me wrong. God saved me from myself. He saved my life by allowing me to go to prison. Maybe he knew that I didn't have the insight to make it to where I am today without divine intervention.

If I had not gone to prison, I could have ended up like Baldy and Son, dying as a result of the drug trade. Perhaps Julio would have finally got the jump on me and ended my life. Still, twenty-four years, seven months, and twenty days is a long time to soak for something you didn't do. I am a free man now as I should be. My past is exactly that, my past. I'm embracing what is in front of me. I don't waste time wondering about what could have been nor do I long to get back the years I spent in prison. God has a way of redeeming the time and making your latter days greater than your former days.

The number seven symbolizes completion and the number eight stands for new beginnings or resurrection. These seven chapters mark the completion of a cycle that was God-ordained. The upcoming eighth chapter of my life is a time of newness. I can't waste my resurrection on what is already done. Now, I live my life to help others because that's what God preserved me all those years to do.

*If you are seeking help with your case, or if you are newly released from prison and need help, contact the following:*

### Jonathan Fleming Foundation
*pjohnson@jf14.org*
*jonathanfleming@jf14.org*

*INVESTIGATORS*
### Bob Rahn
*(845) 662-4272*

### Kim Aklin
*(845) 222-6066*

*ATTORNEY*
### Anthony Mayol
*(718) 909-8538*
*(718) 520-8271*